DON'T GET SICK

The Hidden Dangers of
Camping and Hiking

DON'T GET SICK

SICK

The Hidden Dangers of Camping and Hiking

Buck Tilton, M.S.
& Rick Bennett, Ph.D.

THE MOUNTAINEERS BOOKS

Published by
The Mountaineers Books
1001 SW Klickitat Way, Suite 201
Seattle, WA 98134

First edition (originally titled *Camping Healthy: Hygiene for the Outdoors*), 1995. Second edition, 2002.

Published simultaneously in Great Britain by Cordee, 3a DeMontfort Street, Leicester, England, LE1 7HD

Manufactured in Canada

Project Editor: Christine Ummel Hosler
Copyeditor: Kris Fulsaas
Cover and book design: Ani Rucki
Layout: Hargrave Design
Illustrator: Moore Creative Designs
Cover illustration: Ani Rucki

Library of Congress Cataloging-in-Publication Data
Tilton, Buck.
    Don't get sick : the hidden dangers of camping and hiking / by Buck
Tilton and Rick Bennett.— 2nd ed.
        p. cm.
    Rev. ed. of: Camping healthy. c1995.
    Includes bibliographical references.
    ISBN 0-89886-854-8 (pbk.)
    1. Camping—Health aspects. 2. Camping injuries. I. Bennett, Rick,
Ph.D. II. Tilton, Buck. Camping healthy. III. Title.
RC88.9.C3 T54 2002
613.6'7—dc21   2001006483

 Printed on recycled paper

To my dad and mom, Jim and Eris Tilton,
who still hope someday I will clean up my act.
—Buck Tilton

To all the great practitioners of applied microbiology who
have ventured into the wilderness of ignorance and
poverty to apply their knowledge in order to lessen the
suffering caused by food- and waterborne disease.
—Rick Bennett

Contents

Introduction   9
    What Are Germs?   10
    Diseases Old and New   10
    What's Wilderness Got to Do With It?   12

Chapter 1. Food- and Waterborne Diseases   14
    Germs That Cause Disease in Humans   16
    Prevention of Communicable Diseases   30

Chapter 2. Sanitizers and How They Work   37
    Halogens   39
    Quaternary Ammonium Compounds   42
    Chlorhexidine Gluconate (CHG)   43
    Hot Water   43

Chapter 3. Keeping Yourself Clean   44
    Hand Washing   44
    Body Washing   49

Chapter 4. Disinfecting Water   51
    Boiling   51
    Halogenation   53
    Filtration   57

Chapter 5. Choosing and Managing Food   60
    Choosing Food   61
    Safe Food Handling and Preparation   63
    Handling Leftovers   64

Chapter 6. **Disposing of Human Waste** 65
    Solid Waste Disposal 65
    Urine Disposal 72

Chapter 7. **Maintaining a Healthy Camp** 74
    The Environmentally Safe Backcountry Camp 74
    Backcountry Kitchen Cleanup 76
    Sharing Is Not Always Caring 78
    Managing Backcountry Trash 79

Chapter 8. **Special Considerations for Groups** 81
    Hazard Analysis and Critical Control Points 81
    Managing Large Groups 82
    Managing Groups with Special Needs 84

Chapter 9. **Diseases Carried by Animals** 87
    Diseases Carried by Ticks 88
    Diseases Carried by Larger Animals 93

Selected References 106

Introduction

> *The goal of this book is to provide the knowledge—some science tempered with common sense—that will make your wilderness trips as totally healthy as possible.*

You have heard the "Call of the Wild." It is a clarion summons, rich with promise. Into your backpack or dry bag, after a bit of contemplative thought, goes the gear you will need—and you are off for a night, a week, or more. Often it takes only the first step on the trail or the initial stroke of the paddle before you begin to feel what you came for: the stirring of adventure, the solace of wild places, the beauty that soars straight to the heart. The exercise is good for the body. The change is good for the mind. The peace is good for the soul.

Beyond your dreams, the campsite you select will remain among the most memorable—an outstanding view, a flow of crystalline water, a tent snuggled in fragrant trees on thick forest duff. Your dinner is delicious. Your companions are lively and lovely. The sunset startles your eyes and your spirit. You settle down into your sleeping bag with a great sense of fulfillment. Life is good!

Wilderness travel, however, despite its incomparably healthy benefits, is not without risk. This is perhaps obvious; but not so obvious is the fact that far more common than the twisted ankle or tweaked knee, the abraded elbow or knife-nicked finger is the possibility of traveling and camping within a community of disease-causing organisms called germs. Yet with a high level of awareness and a few acts of discipline, spiced with a dash of common sense, you can embark on wilderness journeys that can be not only enjoyable but also completely healthy. Contemplate this: In knowledge lies health.

WHAT ARE GERMS?

"Germs" is a scientific term representing all the microscopic things that might, in some cases, infect a human and cause disease. These include viruses, bacteria, fungi and yeasts, and protozoa (see chapter 1, Food- and Waterborne Diseases). First, consider that not all germs are hazardous; many microbes, in fact, are essential for your life and the health of the living world. Some bacteria, for example, are required in our gastrointestinal tracts to break down food molecules into simpler materials that we can assimilate. But some are indeed really bad, extracting a huge toll in cost, suffering, and death.

Bad germs! In the beginning or shortly after, millions of years before we arrived, they were here. When we are all gone, they will probably still be here. Everywhere you go, they go too. Everywhere you stop, some of them are already waiting. They are a part of you and a part of everything you do. From the water we drink to the food we eat to the ways we dispose of body waste, from the nose to the mouth to the hands, from the blister to the boil, bad germs are involved.

DISEASES OLD AND NEW

Though cleanliness is said to be next to godliness, improper hygiene and the resulting transmission of germs may put you even closer, having sent more people on to the afterlife than all other causes of death combined. Before wilderness travel was sport and before modern hygiene existed, there was the bubonic plague, the curse of cholera, and Typhoid Mary. For example, the "Black Death," caused by the bacterium *Yersinia pestis,* in a three-year period (A.D. 1347–1350), wiped out an estimated 25 million Europeans and laid approximately nine-tenths of the population of England underground.

We might think those days of unhygienic mass migrations to the hereafter are over. Humanity has had the audacity to think many microbes were "under control," but everyone who can read knows old enemies are returning (for example, cholera, plague, malaria resistant to anti-malarial drugs, tuberculosis resistant to antibiotics, virulent strains of streptococcus-A, dubbed the "flesh-eating bacteria") and new scourges are on the rise (such as AIDS and hepatitis C). For instance, compare the bubonic plague's annual death toll of around 8 million to today's annual death toll from pneumonia: more than 4 million (see figure 1).

Figure 1.
Major Disease Concerns

Infectious Disease	Cause	Annual Human Deaths
Pneumonia	Bacteria or virus	4.3 million
Diarrheal illness	Bacteria or virus	3.2 million
Tuberculosis	Bacteria	3 million
Hepatitis B	Virus	1.5 million
Malaria	Protozoa	1 million
Measles	Virus	880,000
Tetanus	Bacteria	600,000
AIDS	Virus	550,000
Whooping cough	Bacteria	360,000

Source: World Health Organization 1998, Harvard School of Public Health

On the list of the diseases shown in figure 1, all but two are carried by humans and passed to other humans. Of figure 1's list of who's who in killers of humanity, only two may be considered "environmental":

1. Tetanus is a disease caused by a bacterium, *Clostridium tetani,* found in soil. It can be eliminated as a risk by the safe and effective tetanus vaccine.

2. Malaria, a disease found almost exclusively in tropical regions, is caused by four species of protozoa of the genus *Plasmodia,* carried in the wild and transmitted

by bloodthirsty mosquitoes. Only a few cases show up in the United States each year. Most malarial diseases can be prevented by the ingestion of the newer anti-malarial drugs prior to exposure to the protozoa.

WHAT'S WILDERNESS GOT TO DO WITH IT?

An outdoorsperson might think the great majority of germs lurk in the wilderness waiting for a suitable host to pass near enough for an attack, but this is not so. In fact, in most cases the contrary is true: The germs hitched a free ride into the wilderness with you or some other unwary bipedal primate. As more and more *Homo sapiens* show up more and more often in backcountry areas, the presence of humans, even if for only a short while, has built most of the community of disease possibilities. Although you may travel primarily into regions where men and women are as rare as four-leaf clovers, that is no reason for a false sense of security. With wilderness increasingly trammeled by Leave-A-Trace individuals and groups, there now exist very few places where humans' impact hasn't been felt.

The data shown in figure 1 give a very important message: Although wilderness visitors are placing more and more emphasis on concerns such as the waterborne protozoan *Giardia lamblia,* they downplay the risks from their direct contact with other humans and other sources of disease in the outdoor environment. It surely is important to plan for effective water disinfection, but very few humans will be hospitalized for giardiasis and even fewer will die of it, whereas 1.5 million people die each year from hepatitis B, a disease passed directly from one person to another.

"Wilderness Injuries and Illnesses," an article in the July 1992 *Annals of Emergency Medicine,* reports: "The injury and illness patterns indicate that wilderness medical efforts should concentrate on wilderness hygiene. . . . " In a wild setting, with-

Figure 2.
Some Sources of Bad Germs in the Wilderness

Wilderness Activity	Possible Sources of Bad Germs	Possible Diseases
Cooking	Contaminated food/leftovers Unclean cookware	Diarrheal illness
Drinking	Untreated water Contaminated water bottle Unclean cup Sharing a companion's cup/bottle	Diarrheal illness
Eating	Contaminated food Unclean utensils Sharing a companion's utensils Reaching into food bags with unclean hands Unwashed/poorly washed hands	Diarrheal illness, Hepatitis A
Defecating	Unwashed/poorly washed hands	Hepatitis A
Swimming/ soaking	Contaminated water in eyes, mouth, nose, and/or wounds	Diarrheal illness
Walking barefoot	Germs in soil invading through broken skin	Tetanus
Cohabiting with wildlife	Bites/stings/scratches	Malaria, Lyme disease
Caring for skin	Bacteria harbors in cracked/ chapped/blistered skin	Staph infection
Treating wounds	Improper cleaning/ dressing/recontamination	Staph infection

out the "conveniences" of hot water, flush toilets, and options for safely discarding wastes, greater thought and care are needed to keep the germs—*your* germs—from getting passed on to other humans and into the environment. Your safety from disease in the wilderness is primarily a matter of taking preventive steps before and during the time you are in the wilderness. That's what this book will help you do.

CHAPTER 1

Food- and Waterborne Diseases

IMAGINE THIS:

Out in the wilderness, you awaken early with discomfort in your stomach and that nagging taste of bile rising at the back of your throat. You crawl from your tent just in time to lose your dinner. The sense of relief soon gives way to another irrepressible urge from your nether regions, and you hastily squat behind the nearest bush. The rest of the day is a torment: It's one, then the other. Could it have been prevented?

Mention the words "germ," "microbe," or "infection," and people's reactions range from a bit nervous to nervously phobic. Yes, it is true the microbial world is making a comeback—or is it just seeking opportunity in a global ecology a bit out of balance? Whatever the cause, we are not without our own tricks and host defenses. Most bad germs—excepting some disease agents such as HIV (human immunodeficiency virus, the AIDS virus) and plague bacterium—do *not* have the ability to infect and cause disease in every human they encounter. Not all exposure to disease agents results in infection, and not all infection results in disease.

First of all, it takes more than the mere presence of a single germ to make us sick. For many germs to infect, a mass attack is required. Medical microbiologists (an odd and often morbid lot) call it the minimal infective dose (MID). The MID for many bacteria number in the thousands; other microbes, as few as ten. Once a person has ingested the MID, there is no certainty of any particular outcome and certainly no need to get your Last Will and Testament in order. The right number of invaders has to be in the right place at the right time in the right host. For instance, one member of a group on a trip ingests untreated water and gets two times the MID of Germ X; the sequence proceeds like this:

1. The person is exposed.
2. Infection may or may not occur.
3. If infection occurs, the person may or may not become ill.
4. If illness occurs, the person may or may not become very ill.

When disease results, it is the visible, and certainly felt, expression of a battle being waged between the microbe and the less-than-fortunate host. In the battle of the germs, you may be the "host." To your involuntary credit and your ability to survive, there are many tricks up your evolutionary sleeve. Your body goes to great effort not to be a host. This attribute is called "disease resistance," which can be further described as a set of nonspecific and specific factors.

One nonspecific factor of disease resistance is your skin, a marvelous barrier to the microbial world. Witness what happens when human skin is seriously burned: Infection almost always occurs. Healthy skin also has its own microbial army that digests skin oil and produces a protective acid barrier that inhibits invaders such as *Staphylococcus aureus,* a bacterium abundantly present on skin and in the nose of four out of every ten humans.

Specific disease resistance arises from a healthy and vigorous immune system as it produces protein antibodies, and from special blood cells called lymphocytes. These antibodies and special cells can seek out and inactivate a variety of microbial intruders. Most illness of the sort described in the MID example above is resolved by good immune responses.

The factors that come into play at each step in the MID

example above are disease resistance and immunity. This basic understanding of parasite-host interaction can provide the basis for sound sanitation decisions in the wilderness. Your task is to incorporate prevention into the day-to-day experiences of life outdoors.

Maintaining Resistance and Immunity

To keep resistance and immunity up to par, there are several common and simple things you can do before the trip begins and during the trip to swing the balance in your favor, no matter how brief the intended journey.

✔ Keep the appropriate vaccines up to date.

✔ Practice wilderness hygiene.

✔ Get enough rest. Exhaustion compromises immune function.

✔ Eat enough, and eat a balanced diet. Malnutrition is the world's biggest cause of immune fatigue.

✔ Drink enough water. Adequate hydration improves disease resistance.

✔ Control stress. Chronic stress situations cripple immune responsiveness.

✔ Control other chronic diseases. Metabolic or hormonal diseases alter immune function dramatically.

GERMS THAT CAUSE DISEASE IN HUMANS

The "bugs" of most concern are called *pathogens*: germs that cause at least some *pathos* (the Greek word for suffering) as part of their nature. Some pathogens are more pathological than others, and some hosts are more susceptible. Hence, the degree of pathos is a product of the attributes of the germ and the host. Some humans, you probably have noticed, tend to be continuously ill, while others seem to be superhumanly immune.

Microbiologists class microbes by their biological complexity. In order of increasing complexity, the various kinds of microbes are called:

1. viruses
2. bacteria
3. fungi and yeast
4. protozoa and the larger parasites

The microbes that are clear-cut pathogens have some unique biological characteristics that create chinks in their armor that you can exploit to save your "skin." These "chinks" are described briefly in the section on each type of evildoer.

Viruses

Viruses are unimaginably tiny. They require a living cell that they can enter and redirect in order to have the cell structure manufacture new virus particles. Some viruses can survive for long periods outside of living tissue, but most, fortunately, do not.

Viruses account for the respiratory infections that are responsible for approximately one-half of all acute illnesses. Major viruses cause influenza, the common cold, gastroenteritis (stomach flu), mumps, and measles. Some viruses set up housekeeping in the central nervous system and cause forms of meningitis and encephalitis. Herpes simplex virus type-1 causes cold sores, and herpes simplex virus type-2 causes genital lesions. The Epstein-Barr virus produces infectious mononucleosis. Varicella-zoster virus causes chicken pox, which may appear later in life as shingles. Viruses cause hepatitis (see sidebar The ABCDEs of Viral Hepatitis) and AIDS (see sidebar A Closer Look at a Specific Virus: HIV).

According to new biotech sleuthing, two viruses cause

approximately 67 percent of all food- and water-related viral illnesses:

1. **Norwalk virus,** named for Norwalk, Ohio, where it was first isolated, makes more people sick than all other food-related viruses. It is contacted in contaminated food, drinking water, and recreational waters. The infected person sheds billions of virus particles in feces. The particles are passed easily from one sufferer to another by hand and mouth, and illness rolls into high gear twenty-four to forty-eight hours after contact with as few as ten virus particles. Though it lasts about a week, the problems of vomiting and diarrhea are relatively mild, rarely requiring a doctor's care.

2. **Hepatitis A** can be swallowed with some fecal-contaminated foods and water. Undercooked shellfish from water polluted with human wastes has been a common source of hepatitis A. It can spread through sharing water bottles and utensils, improperly washing

A Closer Look at a Specific Virus: HIV

Human Immunodeficiency Virus (HIV) is communicated by blood and body fluid transmission. Saliva, tears, sweat, urine, and stools can all carry HIV, but blood, semen, and vaginal secretions are the most common modes of transmission. A continuum of problems are caused by HIV. Once HIV is in human blood, the human develops antibodies to the virus that will show up in a blood test. Seropositivity (testing positive for a certain antibody) usually shows up four to six weeks after HIV infection.

Patients who have been infected but have not yet

hands (fecal-oral route), and sexual contact between people. Stomach pain, nausea, vomiting, fatigue, and loss of appetite show up fifteen to fifty days after ingestion. Severe cases may cause jaundice (yellowing of the skin and the whites of the eyes) and dark urine.

Chinks in Viral Armor

Although antibiotics effective against bacteria are of no value whatsoever in treating viruses, some antiviral drugs have met with limited success. Most viruses are inactivated by high heat (such as when water has reached the boiling point), sustained ultraviolet light, and effective doses of sanitizers.

Bacteria

There are thousands of different species of bacteria, as well as strain differences within a single species. Bacteria have a distinct cell wall, much the same as plants, but must absorb their food from the environment instead of converting carbon

developed the antibodies are considered to be in the first stage of the continuum. Stage-two patients have the antibodies but no signs or symptoms of the disease. Once signs and symptoms appear, the patient may still not be technically classified as a sufferer of Acquired Immune Deficiency Syndrome (AIDS). For a while, this stage was called the AIDS-related complex (ARC). AIDS, the final, completely fatal stage of HIV, is a sincerely life-threatening infection that destroys the body's ability to fight off other types of infections.

Regardless of the stage of the disease, the HIV-infected patient can pass the virus.

The ABCDEs of Viral Hepatitis

Viral hepatitis occurs as a result of exposure to one of five distinct viruses. All of them produce degrees of liver illness that can range from relatively mild, flu-like disease to abrupt liver failure.

Hepatitis A and E viruses are spread by fecal-oral transmission. In healthy persons, the disease may be seriously damaging but it is not life-threatening. Outbreaks result from (1) ingestion of untreated, contaminated water, and (2) improper hand washing by an infected carrier who prepares food for others. Infection confers some measure of immunity, but the hepatitis A vaccine is very effective and recommended for travelers.

Hepatitis B, C, and D viruses cause a more severe

dioxide and water into sugar as plants are able to do. It is the cell wall that gives bacteria some of their toughness and resistance to drying and chemicals. Being like small, invisible plant cells, many bacteria grow and reproduce freely in the environment. Other bacteria have a life cycle dependent on a source of living mammalian tissue, but they do not need a host cell's machinery to reproduce, as do viruses. Most of these plant-like critters perform essential ecological functions such as the decomposition of fallen trees and the conversion of rotting animal tissue to release nitrogen for plant nutrition: in other words, they are parts of the Grand Scheme.

Bacteria are classified fundamentally by a procedure that prepares them for viewing under a microscope. Bacteria will stain either red or blue in the Gram reaction, a method of staining bacteria developed by Hans Gram, a Danish physician. Red-staining bacteria are **Gram negative,** and blue-

and lasting hepatitis. Both B and C are considered blood-borne pathogens. Every year in the United States, there are approximately 320,000 and 36,000 new cases of hepatitis B and C, respectively. Both diseases can result in long-term, progressive liver failure. The most common means of transmission is a drug user's syringe. Sexual contact and occupational blood contact are other common routes of exposure. Blood contact may be as subtle as sharing a toothbrush if the carrier's gums bleed. Hepatitis D usually occurs as a co-infection with B, resulting from a blood transfusion or transplant surgery. The hepatitis B vaccine is effective and recommended for people who work in health care and large communal living situations.

staining bacteria are **Gram positive.** Bacteria are further grouped by their shape, which is either a *coccus* (plural *cocci*), a spheroid, oval, or ball shape; or a **rod shape** that ranges from very long, thin rods to short, stubby rods that often appear similar to cocci (making the work of the microbiologist tricky from time to time).

Gram Positive Bacteria

The Gram positive cocci include two of the best-known bacteria: *Staphylococcus aureus* (commonly called *Staph*) and *Streptococcus* (commonly called *Strep*), a genus with several common species.

Staphylococcus aureus lives on the skin and in the noses of approximately one-half of all humans; it typically causes little harm until it finds a foothold in the host's resistance. Ugly conditions such as boils, abscesses, wound infections, and pneumonia often result from *Staph.* If conditions are right, this pest will grow rapidly on things such as tuna salad and dairy products (see figure 3). In this case, the *Staph* produces a toxin as it grows, and minuscule amounts of this toxin will do the evil deed in about four hours after ingestion. A "hand-made" tuna sandwich carried in a backpack on a warm day for a few hours can send you rushing behind bushes for six to eight hours with nausea and vomiting severe enough to debilitate you.

Streptococci means "chain-forming cocci," which appear under the microscopic as a chain of oh-so-unpleasant pearls. The *Streptococci,* unlike their cousins the *Enterococci,* are seldom associated with food- and waterborne illnesses. They are usually transmitted from one person to another. The *Strep* diseases are

Figure 3.
Bacterial Growth Phases on a Warm Tuna Sandwich

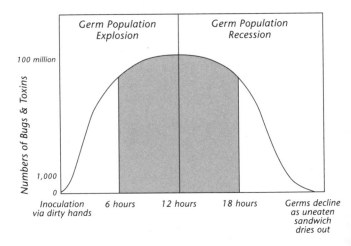

notorious: Scarlet fever took a tremendous toll before the days of milk pasteurization; rheumatic fever, even today, damages the valves of the heart in seriously diseased children; and *Strep* pneumonia is often the real cause of death among humans with serious long-term disease problems of another source.

Many other Gram positive bacteria live in soil (for example, *Clostridium tetani,* known as tetanus) and water (for example, *Bacillus cereus,* a source of mild diarrhea in humans, and *Bacillus anthracis,* the anthrax agent).

Gram Negative Bacteria

Some nasty Gram negative bacteria, such as *Haemophilus influenzae* (airway and ear infections, especially in children), *Neisseria meningitidis* (bacterial meningitis), and *Bordetella pertussis* (whooping cough), cause severe and life-threatening infections of the airway and brain. There is virtually no risk of developing these diseases in the wilderness unless you were exposed before your trip.

Some of the Gram negative bacteria, on the other hand, often travel with you in your food and your bowels. All feces are loaded with Gram negative bacteria. Human stool contains an average of 1 trillion bacteria per gram—almost one-third of the fecal mass. Fecal matter from animals, wild and domestic, also packs a few unpleasant punches. One of the most common potential pathogens in fecal matter is *Escherichia coli.* Some strains of *E. coli,* such as O157:H7, pack a toxic wallop, producing a bloody diarrhea, colon ulcers, and kidney failure. Cattle feces and raw meat are two of the most common sources of this bad bug.

Bacteria in Food-borne Disease

The role of bacteria in food-borne disease is common headline news. In the United States, six bacteria are blamed for more than 90 percent of all dietary-related bacterial illnesses.

1. *Bacillus cereus* lives as a spore (a dry, seedlike structure) in grains and spices, and germinates when the food is moist and when contaminated cooked food is improperly stored. Stomach pain, nausea and vomiting, and sometimes mild diarrhea usually occur within eight to sixteen hours of ingestion. The problem almost always self-limits in fewer than twenty-four hours.

2. *Staphylococcus aureus* may drop from contaminated hands into breakfast, lunch, and dinner. *S. aureus* multiplies with great speed in protein-rich foods at warm temperatures. Rather than causing an infectious disease, the bacteria produce a toxin. The reaction that erupts suddenly thirty minutes to six hours after you have eaten produces cramps, vomiting, diarrhea, headache, sweats, and chills. Although the problem may last one to two days, medical treatment is seldom required unless you let yourself get seriously dehydrated.

3. *Shigella* most often gets into you from food and water contaminated with fecal matter, usually from the hands of the person who last handled the food and water. Shigellosis causes dysentery (bloody, mucus-ridden diarrhea), fever, bad stomach cramps, and a search for a doctor. Illness will probably appear fewer than four days after ingestion, but some cases have shown up seven days later.

4. *Salmonella* is common in eggs, poorly processed or raw dairy products, and undercooked poultry or beef. Within an average of twelve to twenty-four hours, sometimes faster, symptoms appear: stomach pain, diarrhea, nausea, vomiting, headache, chills, weakness, and thirst. Fever may be present. Although cases have been known

to become severe, most people recover by drinking lots of fluids and waiting in distress.

5. *Campylobacter jejuni* contaminates meats primarily, especially chicken, although some types are common in backcountry water and fecal matter. The likelihood of contracting the bacteria increases if you handle raw or eat undercooked flesh. An average of four to seven days passes after ingestion before you get stomach pain and bloody diarrhea. The problem may last two to seven days. Find a doctor.

6. *Clostridium perfringens* and *C. dificil* are found in meat usually stored at too warm a temperature before serving. Eight to twenty-two hours after exposure, abdominal cramps, nausea, and diarrhea may make you think life as you know it has ended permanently. Vomiting, headache, fever, and chills are rare with *C. perfringens*. Symptoms usually go away harmlessly within thirty-six hours.

Other bacteria deserving Dishonorable Mention as possible food-borne pathogens include *Vibrio cholerae* and *Yersinia enterocolitica*. They cause, in general, diarrhea, nausea, and/ or vomiting. In the case of *Yersinia,* abdominal pain may mimic appendicitis. Several less common food-borne bacteria have been known to cause death in the United States in recent years: *Listeria monocytogenes, Salmonella typhimurium,* and *Clostridium botulinum*. Storing food at too warm a temperature, contaminated food handlers, and improper food processing have been the cause of outbreaks.

Chinks in Bacterial Armor

Though some antibiotics remain effective in the treatment of bacterial infections, bacteria, like some insects, have developed unique adaptations to the poisons in their world, making many common antibiotics useless against them today. The problem of antibiotic resistance now poses a threat for even the common and ordinary kinds of infections, and blind reliance on the antibiotics in your first-aid kit is no longer a sound strategy. Most bacteria are killed by sanitizers, high temperatures (as when water has reached the boiling point), prolonged exposure to ultraviolet light, and plain old dryness.

A Closer Look at a Specific Bacterium: *E. coli*

No one has a stool smear that will ever win Garden Beautiful, but every human intestinal tract flowers with a variety of bacteria living in a healthy symbiotic relationship with the involuntary gardener. Normal gut flora for an average person weigh in at 3 to 4 pounds (1.35 to 1.8 kilograms), and include, in addition to the beneficial species, nasty life forms such as *Clostridium, Enterococcus,* and numerous strains of *Escherichia coli.* Most *E. coli* are strains that have little ability to produce disease, but some strains with great pathos have been incriminated in serious disease outbreaks. As many as 92 percent of the seriously ill patients, where the source could be traced, got sick from food stored at improper temperatures and handled by people with poor personal hygiene.

Like most bacterial pathogens, *E. coli* cannot be frozen to death and will multiply slowly even at temperatures as low as 44°F (7°C), but it can be killed by thorough cooking. A major source of "travelers diarrhea," *E. coli* survives well in water contaminated with feces. *E. coli* may be found in a bladder infection, septic shock from wound infections, and a ruptured appendix.

Fungi and Yeast

Fungi are primitive, plantlike life forms that tend to favor moist environments and feed on living plants, decaying organic matter, and animal tissue. Although systemic fungal infections may be serious, outdoor fungal infections are usually bothersome but relatively mild in terms of disease processes. Athlete's foot, for instance, is caused by one of several dermatophytes (fungal parasites that grow on skin): *Tricophyton rubrum*, *Tricophyton mentagrophytes*, or *Epidermophyton floccosum*. Ringworm and

A Closer Look at a Specific Fungal Infection: Swimmer's Ear

During a cool dip after a hot hike, a fungal (or bacterial) life form in the water may take up residence in your ear. It happens when water is trapped in the ear canal. The water is absorbed—readily, in fact—and the ear canal gets swollen and wrinkly: dishpan ear canal. Opportunistic fungi from the water can now invade—and you are infected. The swollen ear canal hurts, sometimes to miserable extremes. The ear may feel "blocked." To test for an infection of the outer ear—*Otitis externa* or "swimmer's ear"—tug on the outer ear. A marked increase in pain accompanies the tug.

To treat the problem, start by cleaning the ear canal as much as possible. Irrigation often works just fine, and may be your only option in the wilderness. Irrigate with warm, clean water (water safe to drink) or, even better, with a dilute solution of alcohol or vinegar (four parts water to one part alcohol or vinegar). If you are susceptible, a quick flush with the alcohol or vinegar solution after swimming will prevent the problem.

vaginal yeast infections are also fungal infections. Fungi generally produce itching, pain, and scaling. In the immunosuppressed, a fungal infection called candidiasis can be overwhelming and fatal.

Chinks in Fungal Armor

Common antibiotics are of no value in treating fungi, and fungi can also be resistant to sanitizers, but special fungicidal liquids, ointments, and powders usually work. Keeping your skin clean and dry helps defeat fungal infections. Exposure to ultraviolet light may be helpful.

Protozoa

Protozoa are a phylum of the animal kingdom that includes the simplest creatures, most of them one-celled. Parasitic protozoa include the four species of *Plasmodia* that cause malaria.

Giardia lamblia parasites swim or float around as cysts in many wilderness water sources and spread through fecal contamination by humans and other animals. *Giardia* is the most frequent cause of nonbacterial diarrhea in North America. Unpleasant but typically benign, the illness usually causes more than a week of diarrhea with bloating, flatulence, and stomach cramps. Symptoms take about ten days to show up, but the parasites may hang around inside for weeks before you feel sick. Some patients never develop the typical signs and symptoms of giardiasis; they have periodic mild cramping and bloating, but they never explode with diarrhea. Some carriers of *Giardia lamblia* are asymptomatic—sort of Giardia Marys.

Another protozoa, *Cryptosporidium parvum,* although transmittable via food and body contact, is primarily a waterborne parasite. The little bugs get in water from feces of infected animals, including humans; young animals, both wild and domestic, are the most susceptible. Approximately 80 percent

A Closer Look at a Specific Protozoa: Amoebas

Amoebas seldom draw much medical attention in North America, with good reason: In these northern lands, amoebic disease is rare. Travelers in Africa, Central America, or South America may encounter this microscopic "blob" and thereafter suffer from serious bouts of recurrent diarrhea.

Not so rare, however, is the increasingly popular outdoor quest for natural hot springs. There is great appeal and charm to immersing your tired body in fresh, hot water under a cobalt sky as cool wilderness breezes brush by. But a number of warm-water ponds and hot springs in North America, and worldwide, have earned the dire reputation as a source of an infective amoeba, *Naegleria fowleri.* This nasty protozoan is the cause of Primary Amoebic Meningoencephalitis (PAM). This infection is very severe and often fatal. The microbe invades the mucus membranes of the nose and then burrows through the bony structures that separate the nasal passages from the brain. In a matter of a few days to a week or so after exposure, disease signs include headache, fever, lethargy, and a reduction of the level of consciousness. This pattern can easily be mistaken for bacterial meningitis. Antibiotics are not effective against this protozoan.

Someone with a history of these signs should always seek medical attention; be sure to inform the clinician that the affected person was recreating in warm waters in the great outdoors. If that does not get a response, mention the amoeba and PAM.

Better yet, investigate the history of a hot spring and, if the status is not known, it is wise to keep your face out of the water.

of the people in the United States have been exposed to *Cryptosporidia*. Explosive diarrhea and tummy cramps appear after an incubation period of four to fourteen days and self-limit, going away after five to eleven miserable days.

Cyclospora species were not identified as human pathogens until 1979. Whether or not they can be passed via fecal-oral routes (from water and soil) remains in question, but they are decidedly associated with contaminated food. Not considered a problem in the United States until recently, outbreaks have occurred, most of them east of the Rocky Mountains. A sudden onset of long-lasting diarrhea (sometimes seven weeks or more) results, and a physician's consultation is recommended.

Chinks in Protozoal Armor

Heating water to the boiling point and filtering water with most filters will rid water of viable *Giardia lamblia*. *Giardia* cysts are moderately resistant to chemical disinfectants, but the disinfectant will usually work if contact time is long enough. Be especially careful if the water is cold and/or dirty—more of the chemical is needed. *Cryptosporidium* are thick-walled and extremely resistant to chemical disinfectants, but they can be filtered out by the same filters that remove *Giardia,* or cooked to death in water that reaches boiling. The killing of *Cyclospora* has not been well studied, but they are similar in biological construction to *Cryptosporidium* and most likely are eliminated in ways that kill or remove *Crypto*.

PREVENTION OF COMMUNICABLE DISEASES

Prevention of communicable disease requires, more than anything else, a change in behavior. Keep in mind that a community of diseases, especially in the wilderness, may be created and maintained in any group by very casual means.

The obvious bottom line in the prevention of communicable diseases is universal body substance precautions with all humans. It is safest to disregard thoughts of "this is a high-risk person" and "this is a low-risk person." Consider *all* people as potential transmitters of infectious disease.

Prevention of environmental diseases relies on awareness of their causes and use of practical methods to avoid them (for example, tetanus vaccinations and water disinfection). The next six chapters cover these methods in detail, as highlighted below.

✔ Keep all your vaccinations up to date.

✔ Wash your hands very thoroughly before and after treating a sick or injured person (see chapter 3, Keeping Yourself Clean).

✔ Carry disposable surgical gloves in each wilderness first-aid kit—and wear them when needed! Contact with blood poses the greatest risk. If the wound is minor, direct the patient in the cleaning of her or his own wound.

✔ Use a pocket mask with a one-way valve when performing mouth-to-mouth breathing.

✔ Double-bag in plastic all soiled bandages and dressings if they cannot be completely burned in an environmentally safe, hot fire.

✔ Wash your hands before preparing meals and after you relieve yourself (see chapter 3, Keeping Yourself Clean).

✔ Disinfect all drinking water via water filtration, halogenation (chemicals), or boiling (see chapter 4, Disinfecting Water).

✔ Properly choose, pack, and prepare food, and properly dispose of all leftover food (see chapter 5, Choosing and Managing Food).

(Continued on page 36)

Figure 4.

Common Food-borne Diseases

Causative Agent	Typical Foods
Nausea, vomiting symptoms occur first	
Staphylococcus aureus and its enterotoxins	Ham, meat, poultry products, cream-filled pastry, whipped butter, cheese
Bacillus cereus	Meat products, soups, sauces, vegetables
Amanita-toxins (amatoxins)	*Amanita* species of wild mushrooms
Lower gastrointestinal tract symptoms (abdominal cramps, diarrhea) occur first or predominate	
Clostridium perfringens, *Bacillus cereus*, *Streptococcus faecalis*, *S. faecium*	Cooked meat and poultry, cooked rice and pasta
Salmonella species (including *S. arizonae*), *Shigella*, enteropathogen *Escherichia coli*, other enterobacteriacae, *Vibrio parahaemolyticus*, *Yersinia enterocolitica*, *Pseudomonas aeruginosa*, *Aeromonas hydrophila*, *Pesiomonas shigelloides*, *Campylobacter jejuni*, *Vibriocholerae* (Ol and non-Ol), *V. vulnificus*, *V. fluvialis*	Raw, undercooked eggs; raw milk, meat, and poultry

Principal Symptoms	Latency Period
Nausea, vomiting, retching, diarrhea, abdominal pain, prostration	1–6 hrs; mean, 2–4 hrs
Vomiting, abdominal cramps, diarrhea, nausea	8–6 hrs (2–4 hrs: emesis possible)
Nausea, vomiting, diarrhea, thirst, dilation of pupils, collapse, coma, death in about 50 percent of cases	6–24 hrs
Abdominal cramps, diarrhea, putrefactive diarrhea associated with *C. perfringens,* sometimes nausea and vomiting	2–36 hrs; mean, 6–12 hrs
Abdominal cramps, diarrhea, vomiting, fever, chills, malaise, nausea, headache. Sometimes bloody or mucoid diarrhea, cutaneous lesions associated with *V. vulnificus. Yersinia enterocolitica* mimics flu and acute appendicitis.	12–74 hrs; mean, 18–36 hrs

(Continued on next page)

Figure 4.
Common Food-borne Diseases *(continued)*

Causative Agent	Typical Foods

Lower gastrointestinal tract symptoms
(abdominal cramps, diarrhea) occur first or predominate (continued)

Causative Agent	Typical Foods
Cryptosporidium parvum	Contaminated food or water
Enteric viruses	Contaminated water, raw shellfish
Giardia lamblia	Contaminated food and water
Entamoeba histolytica	Contaminated raw foods and water
Taenia saginata, T. solium	Undercooked meats

Generalized infection symptoms
(fever, chills, malaise, prostration, aches, swollen lymph nodes) occur

Causative Agent	Typical Foods
Trichinella spiralis	Raw or undercooked pork or meat of carnivorous animals (such as bears)
Salmonella typhi	Raw or undercooked eggs; raw milk, meat, and poultry

Principal Symptoms	Latency Period
Diarrhea; sometimes fever, nausea, and vomiting	1–12 days
Diarrhea, fever, vomiting, abdominal pain, respiratory symptoms	3–5 days
Mucoid diarrhea (fatty stools), abdominal pain, weight loss	1–6 weeks
Abdominal pain, diarrhea, constipation, headache, drowsiness, ulcers, variable— often asymptomatic	1–several weeks
Nervousness, insomnia, hunger pains, anorexia, weight loss, abdominal pain, sometimes gastroenteritis	3–6 months
Gastroenteritis, fever, edema about the eyes, perspiration, muscular pain, chills, prostration, labored breathing	4–28 days; mean, 9 days
Malaise, headache, fever, cough, nausea, vomiting, constipation, abdominal pain, chills, rose spots, bloody stools	7–28 days; mean, 14 days

✔ Properly dispose of all human wastes (see chapter 6, Disposing of Human Waste).

✔ Wash and let air-dry all community kitchen gear, and keep anyone remotely suspected of illness out of the camp "kitchen" (see chapter 7, Maintaining a Healthy Camp).

✔ Properly dispose of all litter (see chapter 7, Maintaining a Healthy Camp).

✔ Do not share bandannas, toothbrushes, razors, water bottles, eating utensils, and the like.

✔ Practice safe sex.

CHAPTER 2

Sanitizers and How They Work

IMAGINE THIS:
You're carrying a filter and iodine tablets to guarantee safe drinking water, but you forgot the camp soap for pots and pans. How do you know whether your kitchen gear is safe to use?

Chemicals that have the ability to inactivate or kill bacteria quickly make life a whole lot safer. Consider the epidemics of typhoid fever and cholera that ravage lesser-developed countries today. The bacteria that cause these diseases, and many more, are readily destroyed by a host of relatively inexpensive and comparatively safe-to-use compounds. Knowing how these chemicals do what they do may help you decide which to use under what circumstances.

One basic concept that seems to get lost in the debate over which compound is best concerns the relationship of "concentration" and "time" (called the Contact Time). Any chemical that significantly reduces great numbers of bacteria has to be in contact with the bugs either (1) in enough concentration or (2) for enough time. So for any chemical that does an effective job, be it chlorine in water or some antibiotic in you, the effectiveness falls along a continuum between a very high concentration for a very short exposure and a very low concentration for a very long exposure.

One factor that determines which chemical to use is a simple matter of toxicity. If the sanitizer (or drug) kills the germs *and* the host, somebody messed up. When sanitizers are used on human skin, the concentrations of the chemical are usually low but used for a long time. Recommendations for hand washing with sanitizers that suggest a thirty-second scrub (instead of a quick rinse) and prescriptions that tell you to swallow an antibiotic once a day for two weeks (instead of all at one time) take this principle into account. There is no point in burning down the barn to get rid of a couple of mice. Use a dose that works, and no more.

Understanding how chemicals sanitize requires a little imagination. Germs are microscopic critters with a cellular anatomy and physiology similar to yours. The machinery of

The Contact Time Principle

Because sanitizers are toxic, their use for water disinfection must keep the concentration below—you bet—the human toxicity level. Using the Contact Time principle, water can still be disinfected for bacteria and viruses using toxins such as chlorine. The table in figure 5 shows the contact time and concentrations needed for water with two different pH levels.

Figure 5.
Contact Time Required for Low-level Chlorine Inactivation of Bacteria in Water

Contact Time (in minutes)	Residual Chlorine (parts per million)	
	Water pH 7	Water pH 8
40	0.3	0.6
30	0.4	0.8
10	1.2	2.4
5	2.4	4.8
2	6.0	12.0
1	12.0	24.0

their cells, as with your many cells, is based on proteins and the complex chemistry of protein enzymes. Enzymes are the directive chemists of the cell. Should sensitive cell anatomy or the enzymes of the cell be disrupted, the cell may die, or at least lose its ability to reproduce. Sanitizers, in general, are chemical cell disrupters.

A healthy "zap" is a 99 percent reduction in the number of bugs. On clean surfaces, this hundredfold reduction of bugs is more than adequate. High-level disinfection for medical purposes is a 99.99 percent reduction, but this is difficult to achieve in the field without high concentrations of sanitizers or very hot water.

Sanitizers can be classed in several categories. The various types have advantages and disadvantages that may help you decide which are appropriate for various wilderness applications.

HALOGENS

Chemicals such as chlorine, iodine, bromine, fluorine, and ozone are great and greedy oxidizers. Oxidation substantially changes whatever is oxidized. Rust, the result of oxidation on metal, significantly alters a shiny new piece of steel. Halogens alter the vital organs and enzymes of microbes. They "rust" germs to death.

Chlorine

Chlorine has the advantages of being very inexpensive and very effective for sanitation over a short period of time at 100 to 200 parts per million (ppm). Its disadvantage is that it works best on clean surfaces or in clean water. Debris reacts with chlorine, leaving little of it to hunt out and zap the bacteria.

Chlorine, until fairly recently, had to be carried in liquid form, especially dangerous if the container leaked. A new stabilized dry chlorine compound in tablet form is now available.

This chlorine complex is more effective in a soiled environment because the chlorine is released from the carrier compound of the tablet on demand. In wilderness applications as a final rinse for dishes and hands, you can sanitize with confidence. Other applications of this convenient tablet include the disinfection of cat holes and rendering portable toilets sanitary and much less offensive.

A Closer Look at a Specific Sanitizer: Chlorine

Say you have used a stainless steel cooking pot to soak an infected finger. Now it is dinner time, macaroni will be the next thing in the pot, and it is getting dark. You are carrying liquid household bleach (5 percent hypochlorite solution). To disinfect the pot, you can add a little bleach to water in the pot and swish it around for a long time, or add lots of bleach and swish it a short time. Both will work equally well in terms of killing germs.

Other considerations include your supply of liquid bleach, the "hurry" factor, and the quality of the surface of the pot. An old, rusted, oily pot is harder to sanitize than a new, slick, steel surface.

Iodine

Iodine is the other halogen most commonly used. Iodine in its simple form and in "tamed" forms (such as iodophors) makes a great sanitizer. Tamed iodines have been the skin sanitizers of choice in hospitals for decades. For your hands and cookware, and for water disinfection, it works equally well as long as a sufficient concentration is used for a sufficient

The Chlorine That Ate Your Gear

Liquid chlorine is cheap, effective, and easily carried in small screw-capped bottles. Unfortunately, little bottles often leak liquid. Chlorine can digest synthetic materials as if it was acid.

A very reasonable alternative is to carry chlorine-containing powders. Although they cost a little more than bleach, they offer great shelf life and greater activity in a wide range of water temperatures and qualities. Most pool supply companies carry powdered or tableted chlorines in the isocyanate formulations. Other formulations will work well, too. And your gear may end up whole instead of holey.

Ecological Ethics

In the centuries-old battle of the germs, no chemical has prevented more death and disease than chlorine. It disinfects water and sewage for millions of people every day. But remember the negative impact of chlorine.

Chlorine is an element, and does not break down. It is very reactive, forming compounds in the environment that are very stable and have some profound, long-term ecological impacts. Please do camp healthy and use chlorine as needed, but use only what is needed and dispose of it high and dry to keep it out of natural water sources. Keep in mind that other simple and safe methods of sanitization—such as boiling water—are readily available.

amount of time. Approximately 25 to 75 ppm will achieve the same kill power as chlorine at 150 ppm.

 WARNING: Iodine loses its effectiveness in alkaline water, which might be found in parts of the Southwest.

Iodine costs more than chlorine, and it stains, but it does not appear to create the same environmental hazard as chlorine (see sidebar Ecological Ethics). Pouring an iodine solution over a rock surface or spreading it over a dry dirt area is a better alternative to pouring it in a hole, because the iodine is dispersed instead of concentrated in one place.

Cat Holes and Portable Toilets

The chemical of choice for disinfecting cat holes and portable toilets is one of the halogens in a strong solution (500–1,000 ppm) stirred carefully into the most recent deposit. Dry, powdered, swimming pool–type chlorines will kill bacteria. Caution must be taken to avoid contact with your eyes and skin. It is just like handling household bleach.

Other dry compounds that could be used in portable toilets include either calcium hydroxide (slack lime) or calcium oxide (quick lime). Both are quite caustic and kill by raising the pH of the contents of the toilet. Great care must be taken to keep dry limes dry. Once wet, they create a large amount of heat and can literally take the hair off your hide (one of its past uses by hide tanners).

QUATERNARY AMMONIUM COMPOUNDS

"Quats" are cationic detergents unique in that they contain no halogens yet are good skin and hard-surface sanitizers.

They kill germs by altering some important cell structures and proteins. Quats were developed long ago and are used to a lesser extent today.

CHLORHEXIDINE GLUCONATE (CHG)

CHG is another detergentlike germicidal compound widely used for hand and hard-surface sanitation. It works by messing up the machinery of the germ cell. It has an added benefit of leaving a bacteriostatic rinse film when used at concentrations of at least 150 ppm.

HOT WATER

Heat, although not a chemical sanitizer, does to microbial protein what a hot frying pan does to an egg. The resulting proteinous glump can no longer perform its germy function. When using hot water, the same rules of concentration and time apply, but in this case concentration equals temperature. A spoon, say, immersed momentarily in boiling water will be disinfected. If you boil water in a pot, the interior of the pot is disinfected.

> ### Health Hint
> Never, *ever* mix substances that contain halogens. For example, if you mix iodophor, which contains phosphoric acid, with chlorine, a potentially deadly chlorine gas may be released.

CHAPTER 3

Keeping Yourself Clean

IMAGINE THIS:
You're now three days down the trail, and your tent partner's hands look like they have been on the trail for, well, three days. Tonight he is responsible for dinner. Hey, it is just good old wholesome dirt, right? Or should you ask him to scrub up before opening the freeze-dried chicken delight?

HAND WASHING

Lend a hand, but not a dirty one. The outer layer of your skin is an overlapping armor of dead cells that protect the living cells beneath. Under a microscope, this outer layer looks like the surface of the Colorado Plateau from 30,000 feet (9,144 meters): canyons and mesas, cracks and fissures. Resident microbes are wedged firmly into the low spots. Some of these microbes are friendly, serving to keep skin slightly acid and resistant to other microbial life forms such as fungi. Others, such as *Staphylococcus aureus,* are waiting eagerly for the opportunity to cause disease.

Hands that may show hardly a speck of evidence could have fingers laden with *Staph;* perhaps those fingers spent time exploring the dark passage of a nostril just before chopping onions and adding them to tuna for a sandwich to be eaten later on the trail. The *Staph* microbes, settled into their new warm and luxuriant home between slices of bread, grow in leaps and bounds, doubling their population in minutes. In a matter of a few hours, a few thousand become hundreds of millions, with maximum population reached in about twelve to eighteen hours. The sandwich may taste fine, but even if a small part is consumed, illness will appear four to eight hours later.

In addition to the resident microbes on your skin, transient germs come and go as fortune dictates. They can accumulate rapidly during the wiping phase following bowel movements, and they congregate most thickly under fingernails and in the deeper fissures of fingertips. That is why human hands account for 25 to 40 percent of all food-borne illness.

Hand washing, even with detergents, prior to food handling or attending to wound care does not remove all the bacterial flora residing or trespassing on hands, but it does significantly reduce the chance of contamination. Below are recommended techniques for thoroughly washing your hands.

 Remember:
Even plain old unscientific hand washing beats no hand washing at all.

How to Wash Your Hands Correctly

For maximum cleanliness, use the eight-step hand-washing process described below. Although it is a lot of extra work in a busy schedule, it is based on research observations and years of experience in the health care and food industries.

1. Wet hands with hot, flowing water (100–120°F/ 38–49°C).
2. Soap up until a good lather is attained.
3. Work the lather all over the surface of the hand, concentrating on fingernails and tips. Perform thirty seconds to one minute of active scrubbing.
4. Clean under fingernails.
5. Rinse thoroughly with hot water (very important!).
6. Resoap and relather.
7. Rerinse.
8. Dry hands (very important!).

The "very important!" emphasis given to steps 5 and 8 above deserves a closer look. Hot water and detergent wash the natural oil, and the germs trapped within the oil, off your hands. Water that is too cool merely shifts the oil around and redeposits the grime somewhere else on your hands. If you want the bugs off your hands, you have got to get the oil off, too. Thus, it is very important to rinse with hot water. But washing in itself leaves some bacteria suspended in those last few drops of water. By drying your hands completely, leaving no droplets or freely mobile water remaining, you take away the chance that germs will flow into dinner or somewhere else even less desirable. Also, repeating the soap and lather is important because the first lather-up removes the soils that tend to interfere with the work of the germicide, which makes the second lather more effective in zapping the microscopic denizens. Sure, it is a bother . . . but so is getting sick.

> **Health Hint**
>
> Save a bandanna exclusively for drying your hands after a good washing, or carry a small absorbent towel. Commercially available towels that pack easily and absorb wonderfully are available in many outdoor specialty stores.

How to Wash Your Hands Correctly in the Wilderness

For most of us in the wilderness, hot water is a pleasant surprise rather than the norm. But you can still get clean hands by using this modified wilderness hand-washing technique that substitutes germicidal soap and a fingernail brush for hot water. It's not better than using hot water and soap, but adequate hand sanitation can be achieved with as little as a pint (half liter) of cold water.

1. Wet hands thoroughly.
2. Add a small amount of germicidal soap.

Figure 6.
The Modern Backcountry Kitchen Tool

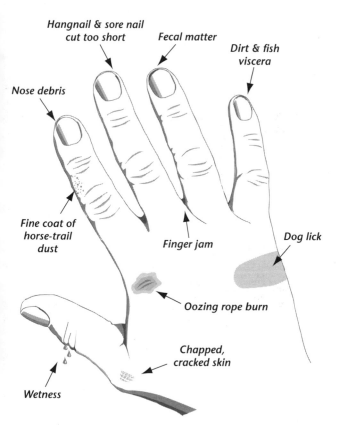

3. Work lather up and scrub with the fingernail brush, especially fingertips, for thirty seconds to one minute.
4. Clean under fingernails (and keep your nails trimmed).
5. Rinse thoroughly.
6. Resoap and relather.
7. Rerinse.
8. Dry.

The germicidal soap kills the transient bacteria where they hide, because the small volume of cold water usually available in the wilderness is not very effective in removing the nasty organisms. The fingernail brush routs the germs from where they are lodged in crevices in the skin (see figure 6).

Preventing Dry, Chapped Hands

Hand washing is the key to breaking the chain of possible contagion, but the wilderness, with or without aggressive washing, can put a really big dent in the "armor" of your skin. Dry, leathery, chapped, cracked hands are almost synonymous with extended wilderness trips. These moist, microscopic cracks and tears in the skin and cuticles become well-stocked hatcheries for a microbial population explosion. Hands in this condition are a threat.

Antibacterial Soaps and Resistant Bacteria

We know the increased use of antibiotics has promoted the growth and development of germs resistant to antibiotics. The increasingly widespread use of antibacterial soaps and some hand sanitizers has given rise in recent years to a valid question: Do antibacterial soaps promote germ resistance to antibiotics? Many experts

What is needed is some good skin care. Many products for outdoor hands line the drugstore shelves, and a simple ingredient such as glycerin is all that is needed to moisturize and revitalize the living skin cells. Wise outdoors folks on more than a one-day or two-day trip take along a small container of a good lotion. Keeping the skin healthy is far more effective than gallons of germicide.

BODY WASHING

On a wilderness trip, germs and filth that collect on the parts of your body other than your hands do not typically create a problem . . . except perhaps social ones. In fact, oils secreted by your skin form a protective layer that helps prevent drying and harm from wind and sun. An exception

> **Health Hint**
>
> Some products advertised for quick hand sanitization, especially in the world of prehospital emergency care, are basically pure rubbing alcohol or are made with rather potent chemicals that are very harsh to your skin. Although these products are appropriate for incidental use, regular use may actually degrade the quality of your skin and promote, sometimes actually increase, the growth of undesirable life forms. If you choose an alcohol-based hand sanitizer, be safe by choosing one with an added moisturizer.

are concerned that widespread use of such soaps will indeed aid resistant strains of bacteria. Keep antibacterial soaps out of your home, and use them only as needed in the wilderness. But, on a safer note, there is no evidence that alcohol gels and wipes as hand sanitizers, despite their harshness, promote resistant strains (see Health Hint in this section).

concerns genitals, especially for women who may be more prone to vaginal infections if their more private parts are not cleaned regularly.

Body washing is most easily accomplished by a plunge in lake, stream, or river—but not in an isolated spring or desert tank, whose limited water cannot easily disperse your grime, and never in any body of water if you are using soap. Undispersed grime and/or soap are harmful to the inhabitants of the water and the environment. A brisk rub with unsoaped hands, however, can remove a fair bit of grime and is probably all you can safely stand when the water runs icy cold.

For a higher level of cleanliness, wash your body with soap; biodegradable soaps are strongly recommended as the environmentally sound choice. Many soaps are available, most often in outdoor specialty stores, that suds up well even in cold water. But even "biodegradable" soaps take a long time to biodegrade, and fish are well known to prefer water to soap. Body washing with soap begins with carrying pots, bottles, or collapsible containers of water at least 200 feet (60 meters—about seventy adult steps) away from any natural water source, to prevent contamination of the water source. Once well away from the water's source, get wet, use as little soap as possible to suds up, and then rinse off.

Heating a pot of water first allows you to have a rather appealing experience, especially if the air temperature is chilly or downright cold. When the sun shines brightly, many people choose to bathe under solar showers; several commercial products are available. Warm water also provides the advantage of easier sudsing.

CHAPTER 4

Disinfecting Water

IMAGINE THIS:
Miles of a hot day on the trail have left your water bottle long empty and your mouth as dry as the Sahara in summer. At last—the musical tinkle of a clear stream crossing the trail! A splash in your face refreshes you. You have never seen water look as clean. It will take time to disinfect a bottleful. How about a quick drink? OK?

Long gone are the days when you could drop your exhausted body to the ground beside a sparkling flow of wilderness water and plunge your face into the cold rush for a drink. Pathogens inhabit, to some degree, most of the world's water. How tragic! And, unless you are willing to risk gut-ripping misery, it is important to carry some means of water disinfection on wilderness trips.

Water "disinfection," by the way, is the proper term in most cases of wilderness water treatment. Water "purification" means removing impurities that alter taste and color, but it does not necessarily mean pathogens have been removed. Water "sterilization" means *all* the microorganisms have been removed from the water, not just pathogens.

There are three proven ways to guarantee your backcountry water is safely disinfected: boiling, treating it with halogens, and filtering.

BOILING
The rule is very simple: Once the water is hot enough to produce one rolling bubble, it is free of organisms that will cause illness—worldwide, and up to at least 19,000 feet (5,791 meters)

Health Hint

Have you inspected your water bottle lately? Does the material in the threads look awful, or have an odor? If so, you might be surprised to find a microbiological zoo housed there. What does it profit you to put disinfected water in an infected water bottle? The bottle needs to be cleaned and sanitized right along with the dishes (see Backcountry Kitchen Cleanup in chapter 7, Maintaining a Healthy Camp). The same admonition also applies to water bladders and the tubes through which water is sucked from the bladders.

above sea level. The reason: All of the time it takes to bring water to a boil works toward the death of organisms in the water. By the time water *reaches* the boiling point, it is safe. *Giardia lamblia* cysts, for instance, die at approximately 122°F (50°C).

The process of bringing water *almost* to the boiling point for disinfection is called pasteurization, for the French microbiologist Louis Pasteur. Pasteurization is achieved by applying heat over time sufficient to reduce bacterial counts by a factor of 10,000—as in pasteurizing milk without a boil. Because all but the rankest water has a pathogen count of less than 10,000, the moment of boiling is a good and reliable indicator for the end point of pasteurization. If you want to "feel" safer, let the water roll around at a boil for a couple of minutes.

Figure 7.
Thermal Death Curve of Virulent E. coli

Temperature	Time Required to Kill *E. coli*
140°F (60°C)	8.34 minutes
145°F (63°C)	2.11 minutes
150°F (66°C)	31.8 seconds
155°F (68°C)	7.8 seconds

Boiling is cheap (the only cost is fuel, though in a winter camp this could be a major consideration) and effective, but it consumes time and it is inconvenient if you run out of water away from camp or during a day's travel.

HALOGENATION

Of chemicals that kill waterborne pathogens, both chlorine and iodine have been proven effective, given enough of the chemical and enough time (see chapter 2, Sanitizers and How They Work). Water temperature, the pH (acidity) of the water, and the turbidity of the water (or, more specifically, the organic material in the water) affect halogenation. Cold, alkaline water and water littered with organic debris, such as dead plants, require higher doses of a halogen to achieve good kill rates. Warm, slightly acidic water and very clear water need considerably less of the halogen and less contact time.

In general, the killing rate for halogens is similar to the killing rate for heat. Higher doses of a halogen work faster than lower doses, but lower doses work just as well given enough time (maybe hours). Lower doses offer the advantage of leaving your water tasting less like a swimming pool. The fact that halogens leave the water tasting crummy is a phenomenon reversible by adding flavoring (such as energy drink powders or vitamin C) *after*

Health Hint

Liquid halogen compounds are convenient to use, and a small bottle of it can last a long time. But halogens have a strong tendency to turn into a gas and drift away—which is why disinfected water smells like chlorine or iodine. The gassing-off process is a function of the age of the chemical and the temperature at which it was stored. Store your halogens as recommended on the label, and start each season with a fresh supply to make sure they will do the job.

the disinfection process has been completed. If you flavor the water prior to complete disinfection, the added substances may disrupt the disinfection process much as natural organic matter in water disrupts the process.

Halogens are generally more convenient and faster than boiling water (when you consider lighting the stove or building the fire), but they cost more and cannot be guaranteed to work as effectively. The contact time and concentration of halogens necessary to kill most bacterial and viral pathogens is easily achieved in the field—but what about those pesky protozoa? *Giardia lamblia* in the adult active form is mostly sensitive to halogens; the quiescent oocyst form is moderately resistant to halogens. The pathogen *Cryptosporidium parvum,* on the other hand, in its common oocyst form in surface waters is very resistant to halogens even at high concentrations. Do not trust a halogen to rid your water of *Cryptosporidium.*

WARNING: Wilderness water drinkers, beware! Virtually all surface water contains *Crypto* from time to time. If your water treatment is only halogens, you remain at risk. The good news is that filters and heat can work against *Crypto* if applied correctly.

Because halogens are effective against bacteria and viruses, you may safely filter out protozoa with a relatively inexpensive filter, then add a halogen to knock out the other germs.

Sodium Hypochlorite (Household Bleach)

Experts do not agree completely on the recommended ratio of sodium hypochlorite (household bleach) to water. There are many variables that influence the kill rate. But we know it works. It is what most city water systems use for disinfection. And we know it is very inexpensive. The procedure to be followed is usually written on the label. When the necessary procedure is

City *Crypto*, Country *Crypto*

Cryptosporidium parvum contaminated the water of 400,000 people in Milwaukee, Wisconsin, in 1993. Stormwater flooded farms and the city water treatment plant. The epidemic of cryptosporidiosis caused a diarrhea crisis. Stores were depleted of bottled water and toilet paper. The city was not protected at all by the routine chlorination of water. Researchers at the U.S. Department of Agriculture exposed *Crypto* to straight bleach for twelve to twenty-four hours and found, much to their amazement, that the protozoan was not affected by undiluted laundry bleach.

not given, look on the label for the percentage of available chlorine (strength of the bleach) and use the information in figure 8 as a guide. If the strength is unknown, add 10 drops per quart (or liter) of clear water. Double the amount of chlorine for cloudy or colored water.

Figure 8.
Sodium Hypochlorite (Household Bleach) to Water

Strength of Available Chlorine	Quart (Liter) of Clear Water
1 percent solution	10 drops
4–6 percent solution	2 drops
7–10 percent solution	1 drop

Mix the treated water thoroughly and allow it to stand for thirty minutes. The water should have a slight chlorine odor—if not, repeat the dosage and allow the water to stand for an additional fifteen minutes. If the treated water has too strong a chlorine taste, it can be made more pleasing by allowing the water to stand exposed to the air for a few hours (gassing off) or by pouring it from one clean container to another several times (aeration).

Calcium Hypochlorite (Granular)

High-test granular calcium hypochlorite has available chlorine equal to 70 percent of its weight. Create a solution from the granular form by dissolving 1 heaping teaspoon of calcium hypochlorite (approximately 1/4 ounce/7 grams) in 2 gallons (7.6 liters) of disinfected water. The mixture will produce a stock chlorine solution of approximately 500 parts per million (500 milligrams per liter). To disinfect water, add the chlorine solution in the ratio of 1 part chlorine solution to each 100 parts water to be treated. This is roughly equal to adding 1 pint (16 ounces/0.5 liter) of stock chlorine solution to each 12.5 gallons (45.4 liters) of water to be disinfected. To remove any objectionable chlorine odor, aerate the water as described in the section on Sodium Hypochlorite, above.

Chlorine (Tablets)

Commercially prepared chlorine tablets containing the necessary dosage for drinking water disinfection can be purchased from drugstores and sporting goods stores. The chemical composition and dosage vary among these products; use as stated in the instructions. When instructions are not available, use one tablet for 1 quart (or liter) of water to be disinfected.

Tincture of Iodine (Liquid)

Common household iodine, 2 percent United States Pharmacopeia (U.S.P.) tincture of iodine, from the medicine chest or first-aid kit may be used to disinfect water. Add five drops to 1 quart (or liter) of clear water. For cloudy water add ten drops. Let the solution stand for at least thirty minutes.

Iodine (Tablets)

Commercially prepared iodine tablets containing the necessary dosage for drinking water disinfection can be purchased from drugstores and sporting goods stores. Their forms also vary; use as stated in the instructions. When instructions are not available, use one tablet for 1 quart (or liter) of water to be disinfected.

> **Health Hint**
> Be sure to label any bottle that contains chlorine or iodine so there is no mistaking its contents.

FILTRATION

Water filters physically strain out some of the organisms and contaminants in water that could cause disease. The effectiveness of filters varies greatly from one that removes only relatively large particles such as *Giardia lamblia* to one that removes virtually everything removable. Viruses are too small to be filtered out, but some filters kill large numbers of viruses with iodine from resins on the filter as the water passes through. Filtered water looks "clean," but the purity of the water depends on the specific filter. Read the claims of a filter carefully before your purchase. They are available in a wide variety of costs, shapes, and sizes. Filtration, in general, costs more but offers the quickest route to safe water.

Structurally, there are two basic kinds of filters:
1. Surface or membrane filters are thin, perforated sheets that block impurities.
2. Depth filters are made of thick, porous materials that trap impurities as the water is forced through.

Mechanically, there are also two basic types of filters:
1. Pump-feed filters require manual force to push the water through the filter.

2. Gravity-feed filters just hang there while water drips via gravity through the system.

Healthy Filter Choice and Use

Make sure the filter pore size is appropriate for the intended use. Some filters, for instance, work for the large protozoa and not bacteria (see figure 9). Do not let insufficient filter capacity limit your water intake. A filter too small for a group's need is a poor reason to become dehydrated. Carry a backup water disinfection plan. Machines tend to break down when needed most.

Do not expect filters to work well if you are trying to filter mud. Use the cleanest water available, and/or pump from hard-rock water basins or a pan or bucket in which the water has sat long enough for settlement to occur. More muscle power is not the answer to filtering more water or filtering water faster. Having the strongest person pump may just cause water to bypass the seals without filtering.

Figure 9.
Relative Sizes of Small Things That Make You Sick

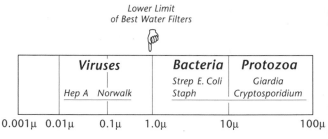

Lower Limit
of Best Water Filters

	Viruses		Bacteria	Protozoa
			Strep E. Coli	Giardia
	Hep A	Norwalk	Staph	Cryptosporidium

0.001μ   0.01μ   0.1μ   1.0μ   10μ   100μ

μ = 1 micron = 1 millionth of a meter

Clean the unit regularly. A layer of algal slime in the filter system is as good as a plug. In the field, store the filter with the input and output of the filter separate to prevent contamination of the output. Keep track of use. Many manufacturers rate the filtering capacity of the filter by the number of gallons filtered. After about 75 percent capacity, many filters start to lose efficiency.

CHAPTER 5

Choosing and Managing Food

IMAGINE THIS:

Your eyes were bigger than your stomach when you whipped up a large pot of dinner last night. With the sunset to watch, the vibrant conversation, maybe a few pulls on the bota of wine, the leftovers, you discover when you settle down to prepare breakfast, were left overnight in the pot. The grub still looks good and smells OK. You decide to heat it up well and finish off dinner for breakfast. A good decision?

Bacteria get into foods in a couple of ways: (1) They are added to the food during preparation or by incidental contamination, or (2) they start there in the raw or newly processed food. Milk, for example, has a resident population of spoilage bugs that will, even with refrigeration, eventually make curds and whey. Almost all dry cereals have a resident population of bacteria seeds called spores, which can remain viable for decades.

Most of the bacteria found in fresh food and cooked food pose a problem only to your appetite. They may taste bad. Spoilage microbes are a critical part of the rot and decay of the natural world that would be a debris-laden mess without them. Controlling spoilage of food on wilderness trips is, however, a tool not only for preventing some illnesses but also for keeping vittles tasty.

Spoilage bacteria grow at a wide range of temperatures. Milk and meat will spoil even at 38°F (3°C). Although most germs with pathos prefer warmer climes, a few pathogens will grow in your backpack on a cool fall day. The notorious *List-*

eria monocytogenes is one cold-loving germ, but serious illness threatens only those humans who are pregnant or resistance-compromised. The chance of a dangerous bacterial explosion in food is influenced by three factors:

1. Dryness, or more specifically the water activity, of a food determines its ability to promote bacterial growth. If moisture is not there, the bugs do not have a chance.
2. Salt content. High concentrations of salt tightly hold the moisture, and microbes are unable to get a drink.
3. Sugar content. High concentrations of sugar also tightly hold the moisture; no water, no growth, no problem.

Drying, salting, and sugaring foods served our ancestors for many generations that never saw a block of ice, and they will serve you today on your wilderness venture.

CHOOSING FOOD

Foods with low water activity such as dried fruit, dry cereals, and dried meat tend to resist spoilage and seldom support the growth of bad bugs. On occasion you might find some mold making a stand on food with low water activity, which spoils a snack. Low-moisture cheeses (dry Monterey Jack, Romano, and the like) can be carried safely for many days. It is helpful to keep them cool enough to prevent the butterfat from separating and making a mess. These cheeses are great for adding flavor to bacteria-free dehydrated foods, and they are a source of high calories.

Salted foods such as dried meats and fish (ham, lox) may cause a substantial intake of water for those humans who consume them, but they tend to resist spoilage due to the tight salt-grasp on the little water that remains.

Choose processed foods over raw foods for your wilderness

trip. Provide individual supplies of things such as trail mix that are eaten out of hand.

Animal Products

High-moisture foods (for example, packaged meats and some cheeses) and low-salt spreads (such as cheese spreads and hummus) are fertile fields for bacteria. Sometimes high-protein foods come "pre-inoculated" with bugs of pathos due to errors in quality control where they are manufactured. Any nondried or nonsalt-heavy animal product must be looked upon with a critical eye. Eating any of these foods after they've spent a warm day in your pack can be a gamble.

Carrying frozen meats on a winter trip is more feasible, yet introduces another concern. For your safety, always assume that raw meat and poultry are contaminated with some pretty serious bad guys. The National Academy of Science revealed in one study that up to 66 percent of all poultry sampled contained *Campylobacter* and/or *Salmonella*. *Campylobacter* is the real cause of what many people call the "24-hour flu." *Salmonella* is much more serious, potentially life-threatening for some folks. The answer: thorough cooking. The interior temperature of a burger or bird should reach at least 170°F (77°C). Because you probably will not have a meat thermometer, cook the meat until all the red is out, and the bugs should be knocked out, too.

Even well-cooked meat may have created a problem: What did the raw meat touch and what touched the raw meat on its journey from the package to the fire? If you put the meat in a pan with your hand and then opened a candy bar to stave off hunger while the meat cooked, you can still get sick. If you sliced the meat and then sliced cheese with the same knife, you can still get sick. Unwashed hands, knives, and cutting surfaces have all produced wilderness trip-shortening results.

If you have not converted to wilderness-oriented vegetarianism by now, you should at least prepare fresh meats with thoughtfulness.

Harvesting Shellfish in the Wild

Many who like to explore the shores of the sea have learned the epicurean delights of the animals that live in shells. Some have even learned to enjoy these bivalves raw, and most of the time there is no regret and little embarrassment from dining on clams, oysters, or mussels. But where human sewage is dumped into the sea, bivalves can concentrate enough bacteria and viruses to make you really ill with *E. coli, Shigella, Salmonella, Norwalk virus,* or *hepatitis A.* The solution is cooking. Bivalves are still delicious when cooked, and cooking takes most of the worry out of a close personal encounter with your favorite mollusk.

There are exceptions. The risk of Paralytic Shellfish Poisoning (PSP, also called red tide poisoning) from bivalves and Demoic Acid Poisoning found in some crabs is not eliminated by cooking. The toxins are heat-resistant, and once you show signs of poisoning, it is too late to turn back. Ask local humans and follow their advice about consuming local sea life. When in doubt, check with the local health department.

SAFE FOOD HANDLING AND PREPARATION

Wash and sanitize your hands prior to food and water preparation (see chapter 3, Keeping Yourself Clean). Use only safe drinking water for food preparation. Keep anyone with the slightest indications of a cold, flu, or skin infection out of the camp kitchen.

Cook food thoroughly. Once food is cooked or rehydrated, consume it. Do not eat any high-moisture food that has been warm for an hour or more. Keep individual eating utensils out of community dishes. Do not share personal utensils, water bottles, etc.

HANDLING LEFTOVERS

Leftovers are the result of cooking more than you can eat, which is a result, most often, of less than optimum meal-planning skills. Storage of cooked-but-uneaten leftovers in the wilderness poses an almost insurmountable problem.

Your best bet is to not eat leftovers. If leftovers *must* be eaten, reheat the food thoroughly. If you opt to eat the remains of, say, last night's macaroni and cheese, be sure to raise the temperature of the food significantly and maintain the high heat for several minutes. The safest procedure is to add water and heat until the water boils. Stir often enough to prevent a burned meal.

What do you do with leftovers that you do not want to eat? Buried food usually ends up being unburied by hungry animals. If campfires are permitted, burn small amounts of dry food, but wet food usually becomes an unsightly lump of ash unless the fire is extremely hot. Leftover food should *ideally* be sealed in plastic bags and packed out.

Successful anglers face the question of what to do with the "leftover" fish heads and guts. Scattering fish parts widely in secluded spots probably rates as the best disposal method in most cases. Throwing the fish remains into cold wilderness water such as a lake or stream is a poor method of disposal because the parts will stay visible for a long time. Where hungry bear populations are dense, water disposal of unused fish parts might be the best idea, however. It could prevent parts of you from becoming the leftovers of a bear's meal.

CHAPTER 6

Disposing of Human Waste

IMAGINE THIS:
*You got the message: Hydrate or . . . well, perish. So you tell
the group you are on the trail with that you need to hang back
a bit and take care of business. When no one remains in sight,
you drop your pack, step off the trail, and look around
thoughtfully for a moment. You cannot help thinking, "Deer
and elk and bears do it wherever they feel like it—so what
does it matter where I urinate?"*

SOLID WASTE DISPOSAL

Human waste, by any other name, smells the same, and you
cannot realistically pack out everything you pack in, except in
special circumstances—such as dragging frozen feces back
from winter trips or portable toilets from river trips. But you
can, with an adequate waste disposal plan, reduce the risk of
contamination (to yourself and the environment) to an absolute minimum. Transmission of fecal-borne pathogens occurs
in four ways:

1. direct contact with the feces
2. indirect contact with hands that have directly contacted
   the feces
3. contact with insects that have contacted the feces
4. drinking water contaminated by feces

Human waste products break down to a harmless state as a
result of two mechanisms: (1) bacterial action in the presence of oxygen, moisture, and warmth (conditions such as
those found in a compost pile), and (2) pathogen death over
time from direct ultraviolet radiation and dryness. Keeping

this in mind, deposition of solid body waste should include thoughtful placement that:

1. maximizes decomposition
2. minimizes the chance of something or someone finding it
3. minimizes the chance of water contamination

If you find an outhouse erected and sustained by some agency such as, say, the U.S. government, you will act most wisely and responsibly to use it—despite the smell. Construction and use of latrines is out, except in pre-established spots. They concentrate too much solid waste in one place. They carry a high risk of water pollution. They invite insect and mammal investigation. They are unsightly, and they stink. If you are ever required to dig a latrine, make it at least a foot deep. Add soil after each deposit, and fill it in when the total excreta lies several inches below the surface.

And, after the deed, wash your hands. Even if you use a thick wad of toilet paper, there will be some fecal contamination on your hands.

Cat Holes

For years, environment- and health-concerned wildland managers have recommended "cat holes" as the best way to dispose of solid waste. It was long assumed that microorganisms in near-surface soil rapidly rendered fecal matter harmless. But then scientists purposefully cat-holed pathogen-impregnated excrement and dug it up a year later, discovering that some of the pathogens were still active. Recent research on both the East and West Coasts, performed independently, discovered that the fecal bacteria *E. coli* not only survives in soil and the sediment of streams and estuaries, but the bacteria actually increase in number to those found in fresh feces. What does this have to do with you and the environment? It means that feces buried where there is some moisture may continue to produce bacteria for months to come. It means your choice of cat hole (or latrine) sites must be well away from seasonal waterways.

And do not assume that the cat hole is going to trap the bad bacteria and viruses in the hole forever. Because some of those pathogens can survive and reproduce for many, many months, and because in those intervening months rain may fall, remember that where the water goes, the germs go as well. In compact, heavy clay soils, even in wet, boggy soils, most bacteria will not migrate far. Sandy soils tell a different story. Viable bacteria can move with ground water for 50 to 100 feet (15–30 meters). Viruses such as the Norwalk flu may be mobile for 1,000 feet (305 meters) or more.

When choosing a spot to dig a cat hole, consider:

1. Soil type. The heavier the soil, the less germs will migrate.
2. Climate. The drier the climate, the less germs will migrate.
3. Water table. The closer the water table to the surface, the greater the chance of water contamination.
4. Slope inclination. The flatter the area, the better.
5. Distance from a water source. Dig at least—*at least*—200 feet (60 meters) from a water source or seasonal run of water.
6. The view.

Once you have sited your cat hole, it should be dug several inches into an organic layer of soil where decomposing microorganisms live most abundantly, preferably in a level spot (see figure 10). After you have dropped your droppings, stir them into the soil to speed decomposition. Do not drop your soiled toilet paper into the hole; pack it out. Cover the mess with a couple of inches of soil, slightly compact the soil, and disguise the spot to hide it from later passersby by sprinkling natural debris or soil over the area.

Figure 10.
The Well-Dug Cat Hole

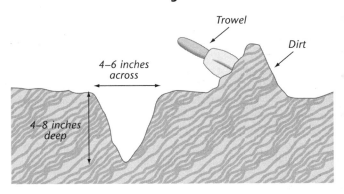

In situations where the soil is sandy and water lies everywhere, cat holes, especially when a large group is involved, pose a high risk of environmental contamination. The risk is not insurmountable; the answer is cat hole disinfection. Dry and liquid sanitizers, which will themselves break down harmlessly, added to the contents of the cat hole and stirred carefully, will reduce billions of nasty bugs to a lifeless mass. Your choice of sanitizers is important; some of them are hazardous to you and the environment (see Cat Holes

Health Hint

Carry a small resealable plastic bag just for packing out soiled toilet paper.

and Portable Toilets in chapter 2, Sanitizers and How They Work).

Surface Disposal

Now it is generally considered that feces will decompose to harmlessness most quickly if you use surface disposal (also known as the "smear technique"), smearing your dung with a stick or rock over the ground's surface to maximize sun and air exposure. Bacteria do not tolerate and will not reproduce in a dry environment. Add some ultraviolet sunlight, and they get a one-two punch. Smears, too, should be at least 200 feet (60 meters—approximately seventy adult paces) from water, and placed where little chance of discovery exists. The smear technique works well in areas where sun shines most of the time and the air is dry (for example, the desert Southwest or the Rockies above tree line).

But the smear technique has obvious drawbacks. For one thing, in well-used areas waste will not decompose fast enough to eliminate health hazards. For another thing, insects have ready access to the fecal matter. In almost all situations, despite a slower decomposition rate in buried waste, it remains best to defecate in thoughtfully situated cat holes.

Sanitation Around the Nation

Wilderness areas, despite the National Wilderness Preservation Act, are not created equal. Some are especially wet, some dry, some cold, and some hot. Special sanitation considerations may be required in special environments.

Lakes and Rivers

Moving well away from bodies of water and carefully selecting your disposal site eliminates most of the health risks associated with water contamination. But in some places, such as deep, steep, dry-country canyons and island-studded lakes, moving well away from water sources is not possible. In those spots, the only safe alternative is packing it out.

The most acceptable means to pack out solid waste requires a commercially obtained portable toilet or a homemade portable toilet such as a sturdy, sealable can like a large ammo box plus several heavy-duty garbage bags. Line the can with a couple of garbage bags folded out over the rim. This is the infamous "groover," so named for the red grooves imprinted in your posterior after even only a few moments of sitting. When the can is not in use, keep the lid on.

Before and after each use, throw in some chemical sanitizers to reduce the smell and slow decomposition (see Cat Holes and Portable Toilets in chapter 2, Sanitizers and How They Work).

 WARNING: Rapid decomposition of feces inside a plastic bag may produce a thoroughly disgusting explosion; the sanitizer is important to use because it keeps this from occurring.

Toilet paper goes into the bag, too, but urinate elsewhere (see Urine Disposal later in this chapter). Urine dilutes the added chemicals and greatly increases bag weight. Before packing the bag for the next day's travel, squeeze your nose shut, squeeze out the air, tie the bag firmly closed, and seal up the can.

Deserts

Human excrement will not decompose when it is deeply buried in sandy, predominantly inorganic desert soil. Bad germs, however, cannot tolerate desiccation and, even though the fecal mass does not decompose, the drying process will be their death. For this reason, use surface disposal. Deposits should be made far from water sources, out of gullies and other obvious drainages, and off of slickrock. Insect contamination in dry regions is low, and smearing your manure in little-used areas rates as a healthier alternative than deeply burying it. Because smeared solid waste will remain visible for a long time, discretion is the better part of desert disposal, and the best all-around choice is a shallow burial. High temperatures near the soil's surface will cook pathogens to death in short order.

Seashores

Cat-holed fecal matter usually decomposes rapidly in moist seashore environments. *E. coli* disobeys the rules: It does not mind salt water and will survive and even reproduce in sea sediment. In less frequented areas, shallow intertidal zones where the water is clear provide the quickest bacterial death. The combination of a little "salt shock" and UV light penetrating the water leads to a fairly rapid kill. Bacteria that encourage decomposition may be one thousand times more abundant in intertidal zones than in sandy areas above the high tide mark.

Where visitors are few and tide pools are absent, depositing fecal matter directly into the sea is sometimes practiced—but it is not recommended. With currents and wind, fecal debris laden with viruses and *E. coli* may wash back up on shore. Your germs may also end up infecting shellfish, which many people harvest to eat. If a sea burial of human feces is necessary, place the mass in a paper bag or biodegradable plastic bag and drop it in water at least 100 feet (30 meters) deep.

WARNING: Fecal bacteria from municipal sewage spills do often contaminate oceans and beaches.

No definitive tests have been run on seafloor decomposition of human wastes that settle to the bottom after being tossed overboard. The temperature is often too cold for bacterial growth, and it is well known that fecal bacteria do not thrive in seawater and will slowly die off—good news, because sealife and seagoing birds are doing it out there all the time. In this case, dilution is, once again, the solution to pollution. In sea sediment and in dark, cloudy water, remember that the story is different. Offshore defecation should always be thoughtfully considered. SCUBA divers, for example, are likely to be offended by it.

Above Timberline
In the frozen Arctic north and in the fragile, oft-frozen high country, decomposition goes slowly due primarily to the cold. Fecal monuments may stand for ages. Here the smear technique offers the fastest decomposition of human wastes; sun can decontaminate and rain and snow can wash away the smear. Choose a secluded spot well away from obvious water sources and drainages. But in high traffic areas, dig a cat hole when it is possible to do so.

Snow
Snow-covered stools, no matter how far they are buried, will appear on the surface come springtime. For that reason, proper choice of burial sites remains of paramount importance. Check a map to determine where snow-covered trails and water sources are, and move at least 200 feet (60 meters) away from them to dispose of waste.

URINE DISPOSAL
Although urine is usually considered a noninfectious waste product, urinating wherever you please is seldom the best idea. Consider:
1. Urine, in some instances, may draw wildlife that can defoliate plants and dig up soil.
2. Urine can (almost always in developing countries) carry

unhealthy parasites such as schistosomes that are spread by careless urination.

3. Urine is rich in a compound called urea, a breakdown product of old proteins. Urea breaks down quickly by environmental microbial action to form ammonia. Ammonia at levels as low as 1 part per million in water can be lethal to many species of aquatic wildlife. If you urinate in small, nonflowing water sources, you could be a death-dealing instrument of ammonial destruction.

To stay on the safe side, urinate on rocks or in nonvegetated spots a reasonable distance from water sources.

On some wilderness waterways, travelers are encouraged to urinate directly into the water. In some areas, this practice is discouraged. Follow local recommendations.

You will cause no harm if you urinate in the sea.

CHAPTER 7

Maintaining a Healthy Camp

> **IMAGINE THIS:**
> *You are hungry. Your cook pot, just removed from your pack, is dark with the thick residue from the last meal and who knows what else. You are wishing you had taken the time to clean it this morning. But it is OK to add water to the dirty pot and start heating it for dinner without washing it. No problem. Right?*

A clean and healthy camp, especially the kitchen, starts before you pack the car and head for the wilderness. Start clean. Kitchen gear, including your pocketknife, needs to be cleaned prior to packing. How many times has a backcountry pot come out of the pack and, oops, a germ garden plot is already well established? The type of cooking gear you choose—aluminum, stainless steel, titanium, wood—is irrelevant as long as you keep it clean both on the trail and between trips.

THE ENVIRONMENTALLY SAFE BACKCOUNTRY CAMP Kitchen

No section of your campsite has more potential for leaving a noticeable trace of your presence than your camp kitchen. Set your kitchen up at least 200 feet (60 meters—seventy adult paces) from any water sources to prevent environmental contamination, and choose a spot that will be minimally impacted by the kneeling, sitting, and walking around you will do during food preparation. Sand and rocks make good kitchen areas. Heavy duff and heavy mature vegetation return quickly to their natural state. Sparse vegetation and fragile young vegetation may be marred for years to come by one night of camping and cooking. If you have to move logs or rocks to make your kitchen comfy, put what you disturbed back where you found it before moving on.

Latrine

Set up the latrine area at least 100 feet (30 meters) away from camp, in a direction away from water sources and any trail (see figure 11), as described in chapter 6, Disposing of Human Waste.

Figure 11.
Careful Camping Protects Wilderness Water

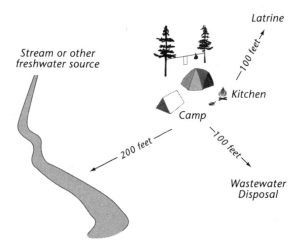

Wastewater Disposal

Dispose of wastewater and chlorine solutions at least 200 feet (60 meters) away from trails, water sources, and wet soils, and 100 feet (30 meters) away from camp (see figure 11).

Chlorine is a very reactive substance, which is why it kills germs so well; at the same time, it reacts with almost everything organic, forming chlorine reactant products. Most of these chemicals are very long-lived and can have significant biological impacts. The best approach may be to cast wastewater high and dry on bare rock or dry dirt and let evaporation do the work. Or "cat hole" the wash water following the decrees of chapter 6, Disposing of Human Waste.

BACKCOUNTRY KITCHEN CLEANUP

Does simply heating unwashed cookware during the cooking process kill all germs? Well, yes and no. Microbes deeply buried in old food will be killed by sufficient heat, but the residual scum left by days of use without cleaning allows bacteria to form bio-films on cookware. These tough microscopic nets permit bad bugs to hide from the effects of soap, water, and sanitizers.

 REMEMBER: Sanitizers work best on clean surfaces. If that pot really does not get hot enough, or if it is used as an eating bowl and an infective dose gets consumed, someone will proably get sick.

Another case worth mentioning is heat-tolerant microbial toxins that can develop in food scum. Consume enough of these nasties, and you will experience several hours questioning the likelihood of your survival. On the plus side, you will recover—and perhaps live long enough to wash your cookware better on future trips.

Cookware and utensils dirtied on the trail are cleaned

> **Health Hint**
>
> On cold-weather trips when the temperature stays below 38°F (3°C), your cooking gear will remain free from germ overpopulation if you allow it to cool off rapidly and then bring your next meal to the boiling point during preparation.

best if they are washed with water suitable for drinking. For the best kitchen cleanup, bring the water to or almost to the point of boiling. Soaps, especially soaps sold for backcountry use (the "environmentally safe" soaps), tend to have less ability to remove fats and proteins. To make the soap work best, you need hot water. Water at 120°F (49°C)—almost too hot to keep your hand in it—will work fine. Water at 80°F (27°C), however, will start re-depositing soluble waste back on the bowls and spoons.

> ### Health Hint
> If you clean as much of the visible remains as possible out of your cooking pot, put it into eating bowls, fill the pot with water, and put it back on the stove or fire right away, cleaning water will be ready by the time you finish consuming your wilderness repast.

You can use sand to scrub clean a hot, soapy pot or bowl, but you will do better to carry an abrasive pad in your kitchen kit—they are cleaner, more effective, and easier to use. Sand abrades soft plastic with myriad scratches that render later cleanings less and less adequate, and eventually impossible.

All washed gear is healthiest when rinsed well with clean, hot water or sanitized water. Recommendations for chlorine concentration for sanitizing surfaces range from 50 to 200 parts per million. Carrying chlorine test strips to assure adequate chlorine in sanitizing solutions is good "health" insurance. Because you are not likely to be carrying a calculator and measuring containers, it will be tough to figure out just how much sanitizer to use for the rinse basin. If the rinse solution has a strong odor from a couple of feet away, it has enough chlorine.

 REMEMBER: *Do not* mix chlorine with cleaners other than simple soap or detergent—the chemical reaction and gases can cause serious eye and/or respiratory injury.

Thoroughly dry all cooking gear. In most climates, the air is fairly dry, and air-drying is preferable to the infamous and not-very-clean camp towel. The towel can be tamed regularly with some soap, water, and sun.

Washing Cookware in the Wilderness

1. Remove as much of the visible food waste as possible.
2. Wash the kitchen gear in hot, soapy water using an abrasive pad to scrub everything well.
3. Rinse the gear well using either clean, hot water or water disinfected with an acceptable sanitizer (iodophors or chlorine work well) at a level of 50 to 200 parts per million. Disinfected water needs to sit for a few minutes after you have added the sanitizer (see chapter 2, Sanitizers and How They Work). Let the washed gear soak in the rinse water for a couple of minutes.
4. Dry the cleaned gear as much as possible.
5. Dispose of wastewater and chlorine solutions at least 200 feet (60 meters) away from water sources and wet soils, or "cat hole" the wash water.

SHARING IS NOT ALWAYS CARING

Nice people are willing to share, but they may be passing around more than their snacks or water bottle. Personal eating and drinking gear should stay personal. If you cannot finish your candy bar or your lunch, dispose of the leftovers properly instead of passing your germs to someone else. Food is usually brought into the wilderness in plastic bags, but rather than reaching into

> **Health Hint**
>
> Food carried in several small, well-sealed plastic bags has a better chance of remaining intact and uncontaminated than food in one larger bag.

someone's bag of gorp for a handful, food contamination can be further reduced by pouring the food out instead.

The same rule about personal gear staying personal should apply to your lip balm and your toothbrush. There is some anecdotal evidence that a toothbrush can spread blood-borne pathogens such as hepatitis C because each brushing usually causes minor bleeding of the gums.

MANAGING BACKCOUNTRY TRASH

As any sanitation engineer can tell you, much can be learned about a person by going through her or his personal refuse. Same goes for backcountry trash—"trash" here meaning inorganic waste brought into the wilderness rather than organic "garbage." In the plus column, the amount of litter in wilderness areas has steadily decreased over the last twenty-five years despite an increase in litter bearers. The potential impact of trash ranks low as a health hazard when compared to, say, the disposition of leftover food and, far more important, human waste products. Still, keeping a clean camp and leaving a clean camp are important considerations in wilderness hygiene.

Start by reducing the amount of your trash at the source. Take your wilderness foods, whenever possible, out of their original boxes, bags, and bulging bundles, and repackage them into reusable containers such as resealable plastic bags. Remove any excess packaging. The less you have to carry in, the less chance you will leave something behind.

Paper may be burned if building a campfire is feasible, allowed, environmentally safe, and ethically acceptable. Be sure you are burning only paper. Much of the "paper" packaging today has nonburnable foil or plastic linings.

If you packed in plastic, tin or aluminum cans, tinfoil, or glass, then pack it out. If you have paper that cannot be burned or will not burn, pack it out. If you see litter left by others, be an extra-nice person and pack it out too. Carry a plastic trash bag with you from home. If you have a designated "garbage can" on your back, you will, believe it or not, have a greater tendency to collect and remove all litter.

To keep things really simple, here's a rule that just about everybody knows but not everybody obeys: If it was packed in, pack it out!

CHAPTER 8

Special Considerations for Groups

> **IMAGINE THIS:**
> *You are the leader—the one who knows the terrain, the skills, the innuendos of life outdoors. You are responsible. And you are concerned: Two members of your group complain of abdominal discomfort and diarrhea. Will it spread like proverbial wildfire through the entire party?*

Excursions into the wild are no longer limited to a handful of very fit and well-trained explorers. Maybe wilderness excursions never were limited to those folks—but today it is common to have large groups, sometimes groups of relative novices, out in the field for weeks at a time. And no longer is the wilderness off-limits to people and groups with special needs. Both these types of groups are worthy of a few special considerations in relation to maintaining health in the backcountry.

HAZARD ANALYSIS AND CRITICAL CONTROL POINTS

In the 1960s, humans began the exploration of an "outside" world of unusual magnitude: space, the "final frontier." The National Aeronautics and Space Administration (NASA) pioneered not only space exploration but also the science of risk management. In that process, NASA asked two important questions: (1) What do the astronauts critically need? (2) How can we assure those needs are met? The risk-management process identifies the hazards and then designs a control system to assure those hazards can be managed most effectively. NASA coined the engineering phrase Hazard Analysis and Critical Control Points (HACCP).

A good case in point was food and water safety for the

astronauts. NASA experts pronounced decisively that illness in the astronauts from contaminated food and water would be catastrophic, not to mention hideous in zero gravity. In the risk management process, they identified the hazard as potentially all food and water. NASA asked what it could do to the food and water supply of the astronauts to make those hazards pose a zero risk. NASA chose "zero risk" because any risk was unacceptable. NASA then developed the control: a process to package each and every serving of food individually, and then subject the sealed container to sterilization. Recall that sterilization is an absolute—no life forms survive. Over the years of space exploration, NASA has had no incident of food- or waterborne illness in space.

Without all the engineering rigor that is being applied to food production systems on Earth today, HACCP can be easily adapted to your wilderness trips. The result: Safer and more enjoyable journeys for any group—whatever the size or special needs may be.

> ### Health Hint
>
> Spare the group from exposure to your germs. Sneeze and cough into your elbow, not into your hand. Remember, your hand is the modern backcountry kitchen tool, so keeping it as clean as possible is even more critical when traveling with a group.

The process begins long before packs are packed and feet hit the trail. A total system is needed, a holistic approach in which the interaction of the people, food, water, and the environment all come together. If you have read the first seven chapters, you have a good idea of how to begin to set up your system.

MANAGING LARGE GROUPS

With each addition of a member to your group, there is increasing opportunity for communication of the microbial type—especially in relation to food and water. Too many cooks spoil the broth—and the health environment. One infected person in a group of twenty, in a matter of twenty-four hours, can infect two more. These in turn can infect two more each, and so on and so on. The result is a large group of mostly unhappy campers (see figure 12).

Figure 12.
The Backcountry Community—Transmitting Disease

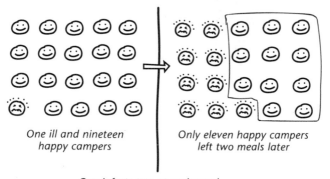

One ill and nineteen
happy campers

Only eleven happy campers
left two meals later

One infects two at each meal

If you are part of a large group, break up into smaller cooking-and-eating groups of no more than four or five people. Each small group functions independently in relation to food, water, cooking, and sanitation. Do not share prepared food between groups unless you take great care to prevent contamination of the food. With the large group divided into independently living groups of five, one sick person may well infect the other four—but because the other fifteen are functionally isolated, the disease can be contained to one smaller group (see figure 13). The concept: Create a "firebreak" within the community in the wilderness to limit disease transmission.

Figure 13.
Effects of Small Groups on Disease Transmission

Twenty campers organized into five-person living groups

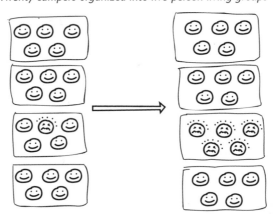

One infects two at each of two meals, outbreak limited to five

MANAGING GROUPS WITH SPECIAL NEEDS

The wilderness experience is healing for persons with serious, even terminal, diseases. Groups of elders can explore and enjoy the most remote parts of the planet. Teams of people with chronic and often debilitating disease and unusual physical challenges enjoy the wild, and do so in a healthy environment. It is not a matter of luck. They are involved with organizations well-schooled in the techniques and application of risk management as a tool to reduce risk while opening the doors to the outdoor world. What does the group critically need? How can you assure those needs are met? (Remember the HACCP section above?)

Consider, for example, a group of diabetics on a wilderness trip. Food selection, food preparation, and preservation of food in a noncontaminated state takes on even greater importance. Effective sanitation ranks among the critically important considerations. What is the condition of the wilderness water sources along the proposed trip? Halogenation may not suffice, and filtration might be the chosen disinfection means. The point: Extra effort in planning and performance is needed to maintain a healthy group with special challenges.

Leadership:
Common Sense Defeats Disease Communication

✔ Do the research. Know well the special needs of a person or a group long before the trip, and make plans for staying healthy.

✔ Always have a backup plan for water disinfection. Who knows when your primary method will no longer suffice?

✔ During long trips, regularly schedule power cleanups. Thoroughly sanitize all group and individual cooking and eating gear.

✔ Lead by example. If you want them to wash their hands, wash yours—often and publicly.

Viruses cause the common cold, and the germs can spread rapidly and easily through a group. But colds are manageable in the wilderness with adequate rest, hydration, nutrition, and isolation (as much as possible) of the sick person.

Other types of viruses cause the flu, and they too are easily passed around. The patient needs supportive care as with a cold, but a bad case of flu can be debilitating, requiring evacuation of the sick person.

Yet other viruses, bacteria, and protozoa give rise to food- and waterborne illnesses, which typically cause abdominal cramps, diarrhea, nausea, and vomiting. Depending on the severity of the illness, these sufferers might be manageable in the field—and it's time to take a second look at camp hygiene.

Is It a Cold, the Flu, or Food- or Waterborne Illness?

OK, leader—on the third morning on this ten-day trip, two people complain about not feeling well. They say they feel "icky." A sense of mild to moderate panic strikes you at the thought of a mini-epidemic. First and foremost, for the safety of the group, keep the sick as isolated as possible: no more kitchen duty, no more water disinfecting duty, no more group hugs. Then try to determine the cause of illness by looking at the symptoms, and treat the patients as necessary. (See figure 14.)

Figure 14.
Common Distinguishing Features of Flu and Colds

Signs and Symptoms	Influenza	Cold
Fatigue	Mild to severe	Mild, if any
Fever	100–104°F (38–40°C)	None to very low
Muscle and joint pain	Yes	No
Headache	Yes	Nasal congestion with drainage
Cough	Yes	Yes
Duration	2–5 days	7–10 days

Chapter 9

Diseases Carried by Animals

IMAGINE THIS:

The cuddly, sweet-faced raccoons that have been wandering into camp each night have proven irresistible to one member of your party. He has been tossing food to them. Overwhelmed by their happy response, tonight he holds the food in his hand, tempting the "masked bandits" to come closer. One does—and nips a finger of the feeder, drawing blood. The cry of rabies rises into the night. Is it time to rush the bitten raccoon-feeder out for a physician's care?

It is a jungle out there . . . or, more accurately, it is a zoo. A healthy camp needs to take into account the fact that you are going to be neighbors, at least most of the time, with wild animals—which means you should be considering zoonoses. Zoonoses (pronounced ZOO-ah-NO-sees) do not refer to the proboscises of wild animals, but to zoonotic diseases: those diseases that can be passed from an animal other than a human to a human. The transmission of a microbe from a wild animal to a human can occur in several ways:

1. Indirect transmission can occur in two ways:
   a. via a messenger such as a tick that bears, say, Lyme disease or Rocky Mountain spotted fever but does not have the disease itself
   b. via the consumption of contaminated meat, such as eating undercooked bear meat, and getting the disease trichinosis
2. Direct transmission is just that; the classic example is rabies. The rabies virus is spread via the infected animal's bite or scratch. The animal has the disease; the virus is in

its saliva, the infected saliva is laid in the victim's new wound, and the virus begins its trek toward the new victim's brain along nerve pathways.

The Good Neighbor Camping Plan

✔ Be selective about your choice of campsites. Avoid obvious animal nests, burrows, and other places they bed down. Avoid places with obvious feces and obvious animal pathways, especially paths leading to water.

✔ Sleep in a tent or on a large ground cloth that keeps ticks away, keeps dust off your face unless the wind is blowing, and keeps other unwanted critters out of your bed.

✔ Disinfect all drinking water.

✔ Keep all food in tightly sealed containers and off the ground to prevent attracting rodents and other small creatures into camp.

✔ Keep your kitchen gear clean.

✔ Wash your hands regularly and thoroughly.

✔ Don't feed the animals.

DISEASES CARRIED BY TICKS

Only mosquitoes, worldwide, transmit disease more often to humans than ticks. In the United States, ticks are far guiltier of harboring zoonotic diseases because mosquito-borne diseases have been substantially eradicated.

Ticks may not attach themselves for several hours after initial skin contact, and in this state can be easily removed. Once they have attached themselves, which is usually painless to you, detachment is substantially more difficult. Because transmission of infection is frequently delayed following tick attachment, sometimes for more than twenty-four hours, attached ticks should be removed immediately when discovered. And, if possible, the tick should be preserved for later identification in case you get sick.

No simple, effective, approved method of causing the tick to detach itself is known. The best method of tick removal is to gently grasp the animal with sharp-tipped tweezers as close as possible to the point of attachment, and remove by applying gentle traction. Grasp the tick perpendicular to its axis. Grasping along its axis may turn the tick into a syringe, squirting its germy contents into you. Do not twist the tick. Do not jerk the tick. Using slow, gentle traction, it is virtually impossible to tear off the tick's "head." A small piece of skin may come off painlessly with the tick, which means tick removal is almost always complete. Every effort should be made to avoid crushing the tick and contaminating either patient or helper with crushed tick material. After removal, the wound should then be cleansed with soap and water or povidone-iodine, and an adhesive-strip bandage should be applied. Tweezers should be disinfected after use.

If you get sick and there is any chance the tick could be the cause, find a physician—the sooner the better. Below are some of the nasties you can get from ticks.

Babesiosis

Tick-transmitted protozoan parasites of the genus *Babesia* cause the disease babesiosis, a malarial-type illness. Although it is on the rise in the United States, most cases, but not all, have been limited to southern New England. Typically, the patient suffers a slow onset of fatigue, general malaise, and loss of appetite. A few days to a week or later, fever, sweats, and achy muscles are common. Most people recover without any specific therapy, but unusual fatigue may hang on for much longer than you would like.

Colorado Tick Fever

This disease is an acute, benign viral infection that occurs throughout the Rocky Mountain area during spring and summer. It is characterized by a sudden onset of fever followed by muscle aches, severe headaches, loss of appetite, nausea, vomiting, and lethargy. There is no specific therapy. The patient suffers until the disease runs its course.

Erhlichiosis

A bacteria, *Erhlichia chaffeensis,* causes human granulocytic erhlichiosis (HGE), the newest threat on the tick-borne–illness front. The flu-like condition is characterized by a persistently high fever, headache, muscle aches, and joint pain. Rashes sometimes occur. Although most patients recover after a depressing monthlong illness, the percentage of people who die is almost as high as with Rocky Mountain Spotted Fever (see below). Antibiotics quickly rid the patient of the disease.

Lyme Disease

Lyme disease is a relatively recently recognized inflammatory illness caused by *Borrelia burgdorferi* bacteria. Lyme disease accounts for approximately 90 percent of tick-borne illnesses in the United States, and the number of cases is on the rise. Areas of high risk are the Northeast, the upper Midwest, California, southern Oregon, and western Nevada. Most cases develop between May 1 and November 30. It takes more than twenty-four hours of attachment for the tick to pass enough bacteria to cause the disease. Early removal means no illness.

The first abnormality is far more often than not an expanding, well-defined red rash. The rash migrates—it fades from one area and appears in another. There is no relationship between where the tick bit and where the rash appears. Flu-like symptoms often develop shortly after the rash appears. Medications shorten the duration of Lyme disease once it is established, and often prevent later problems.

Months after the initial infection, if it's untreated, arthritis may develop, usually affecting the knees and shoulders. Persistent and varied neurologic abnormalities may occur and persist for years.

A vaccine to prevent the disease has been approved by the Food and Drug Administration, and may be available through a local physician's prescription.

Relapsing Tick Fever

Relapsing tick fever is an acute febrile illness caused by *Borrelia* bacteria. Infected ticks, previously attached to wild rodents, are the prime vectors for this disease. Clinically, initial symptoms are those of an acute flu-like illness, but bouts continue at weekly intervals. The diagnosis is established by identification of the organism in blood smears. Antibiotics knock the bugs down. Prophylactically, one should avoid staying in rodent-infested areas, especially in old abandoned cabins anywhere ticks are common.

Rocky Mountain Spotted Fever

In many areas of the United States (especially Montana, Oklahoma, Missouri, and the Carolinas), ticks can transmit a unique bacteria of the genus *Rickettsia,* causing Rocky Mountain spotted fever, an illness characterized initially by fever, headache, sensitivity to bright light, and muscle aches. On the third to fourth day of fever, a pink rash usually appears and may cover a large percentage of the body. If not treated promptly with antibiotics, the disease may be lethal. Rocky Mountain spotted fever is indeed the most fatal tick-borne disease in the United States.

Tick Paralysis

Tick paralysis begins with leg weakness. An ascending, flaccid paralysis follows, which progressively worsens as long as the tick is attached to the patient (usually a child). Speech dysfunction and difficulty swallowing are late signs, and death from aspiration or respiratory paralysis may occur. Removal of the tick results in a progressive return to normal neurologic function. Both diagnostically and therapeutically, early meticulous examination for embedded ticks is mandatory.

Tularemia

Since 1967, fewer than 200 cases of tularemia per year have been diagnosed in the United States. Though certainly once this was a disease associated with unhealthy contact with rabbits, ticks are now, by far, considered the prime transmission mode for this bacteria. Although many species of ticks have been incriminated, dog ticks and lone star ticks rank as the most common reservoirs. Because the infecting organisms have not been found in tick saliva, it is thought they are carried in tick feces. (Rabbits still qualify as the second most common vector, but you must handle infected tissue, as you might do by skinning and eviscerating the animal. Wearing rubber gloves prevents transmission. You could also very rarely pick the disease up in water or soil by direct contact with, ingestion of, or breathing contaminated dust or water particles.)

About 80 percent of tularemia cases appear as red bumps that harden and ulcerate, usually on the lower extremities where the tick bit. Ulcers are typically painful and tender. Enlarged, tender lymph nodes are common. The second most common form of tularemia, the typhoidal form, causes fever, chills, and debility. Weight loss may be significant. Pneumonia is a relatively common complication of tularemia. The treatment of choice is antibiotics.

Preventing Tick Bites in Tick Country

✔ Do not camp in places where you know ticks are running rampant.

✔ Avoid contact with brush whenever possible.

✔ Wear light-colored clothing. Wear long-sleeved shirts and long pants tucked inside a pair of high socks.

✔ Apply a permethrin-based tick repellent to clothing prior to exposure, with particular attention to the ends of shirt sleeves and pants, and about the collar area.

✔ Apply a repellent containing DEET (a concentration of no greater than 35 percent is recommended) to exposed areas of skin.

✔ Perform twice-daily (morning and evening), full-body inspection for ticks—and immediately remove all free-ranging and embedded ticks. The tick seen early is the tick picked off before it finds your blood.

DISEASES CARRIED BY LARGER ANIMALS

You, the outdoorsperson, do *not* rank high as an opportunity for most zoonoses—unless you are a hunter or, for some other reason, you find yourself handling wild animal blood, viscera, secretions, and excretions—but the incidence of several animal diseases, including rabies and plague, in wild populations are on the rise. Your most excellent chance of getting sick, remember, is from the germs *you* pack into the wilderness. See chapter 7, Maintaining a Healthy Camp, for ways to make sure you don't attract the wild critters that carry diseases.

Anisakiasis

The increasing popularity of fish, especially undercooked or raw fish, recently put anisakiasis on the "menu." Salmon, halibut, and other species have been incriminated. The small worm (*Anisakis* larva) that you might consume will not survive long inside you, but while it is there, life will be that less joyful.

Mild infestations include tingling in the throat, and you may cough up nematodes. Severe cases appear like a bad foodborne illness with nausea and appendicitislike pain. Symptoms can arise within hours to two weeks after consumption. The worm invasion can be prevented by thorough cooking—or freezing the meat first for those who just must have it raw.

Hantavirus

Hantavirus infection, the rodent-carried (primarily mice) respiratory disease, has shown up in at least sixteen of the United States now. All of the patients have had fever and muscle aches, and most have had at least one of a group of other symptoms including cough, headache, and abdominal pain. Sounds like any old sickness, but the hantavirus also causes an acute onset of difficulty in breathing that has led to death for a number of humans.

The virus is in the rodent's urine and, possibly, its saliva and feces. The virus can become airborne through misting of the urine or dust from feces or rodent nests. You breathe in the virus; you get sick. You also might be able to swallow the virus. So far it appears that the virus is not transmitted from one human to another. If you suspect you have contracted the hantavirus, you should seek medical attention immediately.

Preventing Hantavirus

✔ Avoid contact with all rodents and their burrows.

✔ Do not use enclosed shelters, such as old cabins.

✔ Do not pitch tents or place sleeping bags near rodent burrows.

✔ Use tents with floors or sleep on ground tarps that extend 2 to 3 feet (0.6–0.9 meter) beyond sleeping bags.

✔ Hang food out of reach of hungry rodents, and well away from sleeping areas.

✔ Promptly and appropriately dispose of all trash and garbage to discourage rodents from visiting your camp in search of easy pickin's.

Leptospirosis

Although infected wildlife shows no signs of the disease, animals shed the *Leptospira* organisms freely in urine. Human cases, usually fewer than 100 each year in the United States, are often acquired from contact with contaminated water and, sometimes, soil. You can also get sick from infected animal blood and tissues. Swallowing ranks as the primary way *Leptospira* get inside humans, but the organisms can "worm" in through abraded skin and through the mucous membranes of the eyes, nose, and mouth. Outdoorspeople who play in rivers (for example, kayakers) in high-risk areas are especially likely to become infected unless they keep the water out of their mouths, eyes, and noses. Leptospirosis appears primarily throughout tropical and temperate regions of the world, and is most commonly seen in Southeast Asia and some areas of Latin America. Recent cases have been brought back from lower Central America, and it is on the rise in Hawaii.

Numerous types of *Leptospira* exist, but the signs and symptoms they produce in humans are much the same. One to two (or as long as three) weeks after you have become a host to the germs, the first of two phases of the disease begins. Phase one lasts four to seven days and shows up in many patients as fever, chills, headache, enlarged lymph nodes, malaise, and a nonproductive cough. After a couple of days off, the disease reappears in a second phase with a lower fever and a severe headache that will not go away. A spotty rash sometimes appears. Muscle aches, stomach pain, nausea, and vomiting can result in either or both phases. Death occurs about 5 percent of the time, most often in the very young and very old. Antibiotics prescribed by physicians are effective treatment.

Plague

There are several—at least three—forms of plague; bubonic is one. An unusual aspect of plague, which is carried by rodents and passed primarily by the bite of rodent fleas, is that both rodent and flea are killed by the organisms, the bacterium *Yersinia pestis.* Black rats are especially susceptible. In the United States, deer mice and various voles maintain the bacterium. It is amplified in prairie dogs and ground squirrels. Other suspects include chipmunks, marmots, wood rats, rabbits, and hares. States in which plague still exists include New Mexico, Arizona, California, Colorado, Utah, Oregon, and Nevada. Hikers and campers in infected areas are at risk. Meat-eating pets that eat infected rodents (or get bitten by infected fleas) can acquire plague. Dogs do not get very sick, but cats do. There is only one known case of plague being passed to a human by a dog, but cats can pass the disease to humans by biting them, coughing on them, or carrying their fleas to them. In the wild, coyotes and bobcats are known to have transmit-

ted plague to humans after the critters were dead and the
humans were skinning them. Skunks, raccoons, and badgers
are suspect. Sick people transmit plague readily to other
people.

Though several forms of plague exist, the common signs
are fever, chills, malaise, muscle aches, and headaches. Black-
ened, bleeding skin sores appear with one form. Gastrointestinal pain with nausea, vomiting, and diarrhea is common. If
plague is suspected, it should be promptly treated with antibiotics. Fatalities are common. Prevention includes avoidance
of rodents, avoiding touching sick or dead animals, and re-
straining dogs and cats while traveling in infected areas.

Rabies

Of the multithousands of humans who die annually from rabies, only a few are in the United States: eighteen documented
cases since 1980, and ten of those acquired the rabies virus
on trips to foreign lands. Over the past twenty years, the number of cases of rabies in domestic animals has steadily dropped,
due primarily to animal vaccination programs. Though rabies
is often thought of as a disease of carnivores, any mammal can
theoretically have it, and cows are the most common domestic animal to carry the disease. Despite the publicity that mad
dogs have received, rabid cats outnumber rabid dogs, with
290 infected cats being destroyed in 1994, and 182 infected
dogs. But the last two decades have shown a steady *increase*
in the number of wild animals having the rabies virus. To con-
fuse things, some animals have dumb (paralytic) rabies, carrying the virus while appearing restless and sick, instead of
exhibiting the snarling, slobbering Cujo form of the disease
called furious rabies.

Just because you get bitten does not mean you will get
sick. Not every animal that has rabies transmits it. On the high

end of estimates, 80 percent of the rabid animals that might bite you will give you the disease. The others do not have enough of the virus in their saliva. Skunks tend to be especially dangerous, secreting more of the virus over a longer period of time, and hanging on tenaciously when they do bite. Of course, smelly considerations keep most humans out of skunk-bite range. Raccoons, conversely, tend to appear cute, cuddly, and approachable, but they can be very deadly. Small rodents such as woodchucks die of rabies, but rarely if ever secrete the virus in their saliva. People who work with animals often get a pre-exposure immunization. It is highly effective, but requires a booster soon after the bite. Failure to be boosted can be fatal.

Just because you do not get bitten does not mean you will not get sick. Infection can occur when saliva contacts open wounds or mucosal membranes (such as your nose and mouth). The lick of a dying dog could kill you. Humans have gotten rabies from breathing the virus in bat-ridden caves where tons of bat saliva and excretions collect. Because the paws and claws of infected animals have sometimes been contaminated by grooming activities, rabies has also been transmitted by a scratch.

Since rabies causes no reaction until it reaches the central nervous system, you do not know you are infected until it is too late to save you. Once replication of the virus starts in the brain, nasty deaths have invariably resulted. If you are bitten by a rabid animal, your life expectancy depends on where the teeth sank in. In rare cases, it has taken a year for the virus to reach an infected human's central nervous system. Usually it takes about sixty days for the virus to reach your brain after a bite on the lower leg, but only about twenty days from a bite on the face. Bites on the hands fall in between. So a bite on the nose should send you looking for a doctor faster than a bite on the toe.

Appropriate and immediate care of the wound is extremely important. Rabies viruses die quickly when exposed to sunlight (ultraviolet radiation), dry air, heat, and detergents. Bites from suspect animals should be washed aggressively as soon as possible with soap and water and/or disinfected with povidone-iodine. If the biting animal can be safely captured or killed and taken, head intact, to the nearest public health department, it can be either watched for signs of rabies or tested for rabies. Testing requires some of the animal's brain tissue . . . which requires killing the live-captured animal. If you cannot obtain conclusive lab tests, bites from wild raccoons, skunks,

Ways to Guess You Have Rabies

✔ The incidence of rabies in the species that bit you. Domestic dogs and cats, ferrets, mice, and rabbits, for instance, are low risk. Raccoons and skunks are high risk.

✔ The behavior of the animal that bit you. Most wild animals intelligently run away from humans. An unprovoked attack might mean rabies. A raccoon, skunk, fox, or bat wandering around in full daylight shows abnormal and suspect behavior. Foaming at the mouth shows up in about half the cases.

✔ The vaccination status of the animal that bit you. Vaccination of domestic animals does not guarantee protection, but it lowers the risk substantially.

✔ Your vaccination status. The immunization is highly effective, but requires a booster soon after the bite.

bats, coyotes, bobcats, and other carnivores should be considered rabid, and you should get the shots that prevent rabies from developing.

Early symptoms of rabies are too general to cause concern: fatigue, headache, irritability, depression, nausea, fever, stomach pain. Sounds like another day at the office. There is only one way to know for sure if you have the disease; unfortunately, the proof results in your death. There are ways to guess you have the virus ambling around inside you, in which case you will want to get the shots that kill the virus particles before they reach your brain. Later symptoms of rabies are wild hallucinations, including episodes of unexplainable terror; extremely painful difficulty in swallowing, to the point of refusing all liquids and drooling constantly ("hydrophobia"); frequent muscle spasms, especially in the face and neck; and, toward the end, complete disorientation and a raging fever. These late signs are the death sentence.

Trichinosis

The parasitic worm *Trichinella spiralis'* larvae, encysted in skeletal muscle, are transmitted when an animal eats infected meat. In the animal's small intestine, the worms mature and mate within a few days, usually within forty-eight hours. Female worms deposit larvae in nearby mucosal tissue. Larvae enter the animal's circulatory system and invade skeletal muscle. Within three weeks, the larvae are encysted and ready to be infectiously passed should anything eat the muscle of the animal that ate the muscle of the animal that had encysted larvae.

Although all carnivorous or omnivorous mammals may have trichinosis, consumption of raw or undercooked pork accounts for the vast majority of the disease in humans. Rodents are often infected, but mice and rats seldom grace a human diet. Bears, raccoons, opossums, seals, walruses, peccaries, and wild swine are common hosts, and sometimes are eaten by humans.

Trichinosis produces gastrointestinal symptoms during the first week after ingestion of infected meat: pain, nausea, vomiting, variable diarrhea. During the second week, as the larvae migrate around your body, capillary damage occurs, commonly producing facial swelling. Migrating larvae can invade the pulmonary system, causing a cough and chest pain, or the heart muscle, causing a chance of death. Gastrointestinal symptoms may remain for four to six weeks, until the worms are all excreted. As the larvae encyst in muscle tissue, significant muscle aches and stiffness often result. Between six and eighteen months after ingestion, the larvae die and become calcified. This period is usually asymptomatic.

No drug exists for safe and effective treatment. Supportive treatment is indicated until the disease has its way with you. Prevention consists of cooking meat until it reaches at least 150°F (66°C), which kills the parasite. Most *Trichinella* larvae are also killed by freezing if the meat is frozen long enough. Holding meat at minus 20° F (minus 4°C) for 6 to 12 days ends the life of the larvae. Warmer freezing temperatures require longer freezer time.

Figure 15.

Animal Diseases That Can Infect Humans

Disease	Common Source	Symptoms
Viral Diseases		
Encephalitis	Horses, rodents	Lethargy, fever, headache, disorientation
Rabies	Cats, dogs, raccoons, skunks, bats, foxes	Fever, headache, agitation, confusion, seizures, excessive salivation, death
Bacterial Diseases		
Campylobacter (a cholera-like illness)	Cattle, sheep, pigs, dogs, rodents, poultry	Acute gastroenteritis, nausea, headache, diarrhea
Cat-scratch diseases	Cats, dogs	Fever, primary skin papule, regional lymph node swelling
Salmonellosis	Cattle, cats, dogs, horses, poultry, turtles	Chills, fever, headache, diarrhea, vomiting
Chlamydial Diseases		
Psittacosis (Ornithosis)	Pigeons, turkeys, parakeets, parrots	Fever, headache, pneumonia

Mode of Acquisition	Prevention
Mosquito or tick bite	Wear protective clothing, insect repellents
Animal bite; contact with infected tissue, body fluids, or feces	Avoid contact with suspected animals; local wound care, pre- and post- exposure immunization/vaccination
Direct contact with food contaminated with animal feces	Avoid contact with infected animals and feces-contaminated food
Direct contact with infected animals	Avoid animal scratches and puncture wounds
Direct contact with animal or its feces; food contamination from infected animals	Improve food processing and preparation
Inhaled from infected birds, carcasses, secretions, and contaminated facilities	Avoid contact with infected birds; control disease with antibiotics

(Continued on next page)

Figure 15.
Animal Diseases That Can Infect Humans *(continued)*

Disease	Common Source	Symptoms
Fungal Diseases		
Ringworm	Cats, cattle	Skin lesions
Parasitic Diseases		
Scabies	Dogs, raccoons	Itching skin lesions
Tosocariasis (Visceral larval migrans)	Dogs, raccoons, cats	Eye disease, brain disease
Toxoplasmosis	Cats, sheep, undercooked meat	Fever, lymphadenopathy, miscarriage, stillbirth, mental retardation

Mode of Acquisition	Prevention
Direct contact with infected animals	Avoid close contact with infected animals; children and individuals with suppressed immune system more susceptible
Direct contact with infected animals	Treat pets; avoid contact with infected animals
Ingestion and contact with infected ovum of parasites	Treat pets; avoid fecal contaminated soil and sandboxes
Ingestion of infected meats, oocysts in fecal contaminated soil	Properly dispose of cat feces; cook meat well; avoid contaminated soil (especially pregnant women and immune-compromised individuals)

Selected References

CHAPTER 1. FOOD- AND WATERBORNE DISEASES

Benenson, Abram S., ed. *Control of Communicable Diseases in Man.* 15th ed. Washington, D.C.: American Public Health Association, 1990. A comprehensive look at all the diseases passed from one human to another.

U.S. Food and Drug Administration. *Bad Bug Book 2001.* Washington, D.C.: U.S. Food and Drug Administration, 2001. Provides basic facts regarding food-borne pathogenic microorganisms and natural toxins, bringing together in one place a comprehensive listing of the microbes and toxins that cause food-borne illness. Available on the web at *http://vm.cfsan.fda.gov/~mow /intro.html.*

World Health Organization. *Removing Obstacles to Healthy Development 2000.* Geneva, Switzerland: World Health Organization, 2000. A gripping report on the impact of the common infectious diseases on the health of the world's population; ample documentation for the seriousness of infectious disease, especially in developing countries. Available on the web at *www.who.int/infectious-disease-report/index-rpt99.html.*

CHAPTER 3. KEEPING YOURSELF CLEAN

McGivney, Annette. *Leave No Trace: A Guide to the New Wilderness Etiquette.* Seattle, Wash.: The Mountaineers Books, 1998. Presents the principles of the Leave No Trace program in a highly readable and nontechnical style.

CHAPTER 4. DISINFECTING WATER

Backer, H. "Field Water Disinfection." Chap. 51 in *Wilderness Medicine,* ed. by Paul S. Auerbach. 4th ed. St. Louis, Mo.: Mosby, Inc., 2001. Massive volume written for and by physicians provides technical information on just about all aspects of traveling healthy in the wilderness around the world.

Wilkerson, James A., M.D. "Immunizations, Sanitation, and Water Disinfection." Chap. 5 in *Medicine for Mountaineering and Other Wilderness Activities,* ed. by James A. Wilkerson. 5th ed. Seattle, Wash.: The Mountaineers Books, 2001. A comprehensive book on all aspects of wilderness health and safety with thorough coverage of illness treatment and prevention.

CHAPTER 6. DISPOSING OF HUMAN WASTE

Cilinburg, Amy, Christopher Monz, and Sharon Kehoe. "Wildland Recreation and Human Waste: A Review of Problems, Practices, and Concerns." *Environmental Management* 25, no. 6 (2000): pp. 587–98. An excellent scientific review of the issues of human waste disposal in public wildlands.

Hampton, Bruce, and David Cole. *Soft Paths: How to Enjoy the Wilderness Without Harming It.* Harrisburg, Penn.: Stackpole Books, 1995. The original publication on leaving no trace in the wilderness.

Leave No Trace, Inc. *Tracker Newsletter.* Boulder, Colo.: Leave No Trace, Inc. Periodic newsletter providing current information on leaving without abusing the wilderness environment. Current issue and additional regional-specific skills and ethics information is available on the web at *www.lnt.org.*

CHAPTER 7. MAINTAINING A HEALTHY CAMP

Hodgson, Michael. *The Basic Essentials of Minimizing Impact.* Guilford, Conn.: The Globe Pequot Press, 1998. A concise and readable summary of using the wilderness without harming it.

U.S. Environmental Protection Agency. *Current Drinking Water Standards.* Washington, D.C.: Office of Water, U.S. Environmental Protection Agency, March 30, 2001. A table that provides the current EPA standards for drinking-water contaminants, including microbes and chemicals (the EPA does not approve or test water filters, but this table may be a good cross-reference for selecting water filters and purifiers). Available on the web at *www.epa.gov/safewater/mcl.html#micro.*

CHAPTER 8. SPECIAL CONSIDERATIONS FOR GROUPS

National Advisory Committee on Microbiological Criteria for Foods. *Hazard Analysis and Critical Control Points Principles and Application Guidelines 1997.* Washington, D.C.: National Advisory Committee on Microbiological Criteria for Foods, 1997. A document that will guide those that need or want to develop their own HACCP plan through the process; the plan is generic and can be adapted to fit any microbial hazard.

U.S. Centers for Disease Control and Prevention. *Diagnosis and Management of Foodborne Illnesses, Recommendations and Reports* 50, no. RR-2 (January 26, 2001). A report intended for physicians that may provide useful information for organizations that extend outdoor experience for special-needs groups; useful for physician advisors to outdoor organizations.

U.S. Food and Drug Administration. "HACCP: A State-of-the-Art Approach to Food Safety." *FDA Backgrounder,* August 1999. Provides ample background and rationale on HACCP for those who seek more information and insight. Available on the web at *http://vm.cfsan.fda.gov/~lrd/bghaccp.html.*

CHAPTER 9. DISEASES CARRIED BY ANIMALS

Beren, George W., ed. *Handbook of Zoonoses.* 2d ed. 2 vols. Boca Raton, Fla.: CRC Press, 1994. Highly technical and extremely well referenced; a good reference for the microbiologist or physician; should be available in most university libraries, see especially sections A and B.

Forgey, William W., M.D.. *Wilderness Medicine.* 5th ed. Guilford, Conn.: Globe Pequot Press, 2000. Covers most of the illnesses and injuries that occur in the wilderness; written for laypersons or physicians; see especially chapter 6, "Infectious Disease."

Freer, L. "Bites and Injuries Inflicted by Wild Animals." Chap. 42 in *Wilderness Medicine,* ed. by Paul S. Auerbach. 4th ed. St. Louis, Mo.: Mosby, Inc., 2001.

Gentile, D., and J. Lang. "Tick-borne Diseases." Chap. 33 in *Wilderness Medicine,* ed. by Paul S. Auerbach. 4th ed. St. Louis, Mo.: Mosby, Inc., 2001.

Keogh, S., and M. Callahan. "Bites and Injuries Inflicted by Domestic Animals." Chap. 41 in *Wilderness Medicine,* ed. by Paul S. Auerbach. 4th ed. St. Louis, Mo.: Mosby, Inc., 2001.

Tilton, Buck, M.S., and Frank Hubbell, D.O. *Medicine for the Backcountry.* 3d ed. Guilford, Conn.: Globe Pequot Press, 1999. Provides information in nontechnical terms on the recognition, treatment, and prevention of wilderness emergencies; see especially chapter 20, "Bites and Stings."

Weiss, E. "Wilderness-Acquired Zoonoses." Chap. 44 in *Wilderness Medicine,* ed. by Paul S. Auerbach. 4th ed. St. Louis, Mo.: Mosby, Inc., 2001.